D0196148

How to Influence

The art of making things happen

Jo Owen

Prentice Hall
Business
is an imprint of

Harlow, England • London • New York • Boston • San Francisco • Toronto
Sydney • Tokyo • Singapore • Hong Kong • Seoul • Taipei • New Delhi
Cape Town • Madrid • Mexico City • Amsterdam • Munich • Paris • Milan

PEARSON EDUCATION LIMITED

Edinburgh Gate
Harlow CM20 2JE
Tel: +44 (0)1279 623623
Fax: +44 (0)1279 431059
Website: www.pearsoned.co.uk

First published in Great Britain in 2010

ISBN: 978-0-273-73116-0

British Library Cataloguing-in-Publication Data
A catalogue record for this book is available from the British Library.

Library of Congress Cataloging-in-Publication Data
A catalog record for this book is available from the Library of Congress

10 9 8 7 6 5 4 3 2 1
14 13 12 11 10

Typeset in 10pt Plantin by 30
Printed in Great Britain by Henry Ling Ltd., at the Dorset Press, Dorchester, Dorset.

The publisher's policy is to use paper manufactured from sustainable forests.

Contents

Introduction: the invisible hand of influence

Part One
The art of influence: acquiring influence and authority   11

1   **Build your platform**   **13**
    Influential people: borrow credibility and influence   17
    Influential places: go where the power is   21
    Claims to fame   25
    Agenda control   29
    Summary   32

2   **Create a network**   **33**
    Weaving the right web of influence   37
    Summary   46

3   **The commitment process: building incremental commitment**   **47**
    The hook   50
    Making commitment a two-way street   58
    Building a tribe: belonging, meaning and recognition   61
    Gaining commitment by giving control   68
    Public commitment, private challenge   71
    Summary   76

Part Two
Whispers of influence: acting and looking the part   **79**

4   **Act the part**   **81**
    Act the part   84
    Ambition: the art of unreasonable management   90

Look the part   92
First impressions   95
Summary   98

5   Active listening   **99**
Open and purposeful questions   103
Reinforcement: the coffee-shop principle   105
Paraphrasing   106
Contradiction   108
Disclosure   109
Summary   111

6   Give to take   **113**
Custom, not generic, generosity   117
Earned, not unearned, generosity   120
Measured, not unlimited, generosity   121
Requested, not unrequested, help   122
Summary   124

Part Three
Weave your web: building commitment and loyalty   **125**

7   The partnership principle: become the trusted partner **127**
Treat people as humans, not roles   130
Act and look like a partner   131
Be credible   133
Be selfless   136
Make the most of moments of truth   137
Summary   139

8   Build trust   **141**
Values alignment   146
Credibility   149
Risk   151
Distance   154
Summary   159

9   Play the right tune   161
    Write the right script   163
    Understanding and adapting to the style of our colleagues 174
    Summary   181

Part Four
Seize the moment: make the most of moments of truth 183

10 Pick your battles   185
    Negotiating budgets: the art of budget smartball   188
    Turning crisis into opportunity   190
    Conflict management: cold wars   193
    Conflict management: hot wars, from FEAR to EAR   196
    Assignments and projects   199
    Making a fast start   202
    Summary: style and substance   206

11 Win–win   209
    Focus on interests, not positions   214
    Offer options   216
    Make a symbolic concession   217
    Craft a story   218
    Public private partnerships   219
    Summary   220

12 Persuasive conversations   223
    Preparation   229
    Alignment   230
    Agree the problem/opportunity   232
    Explore benefits and outcomes   233
    Outline the solution   233
    Pre-empt and resolve outstanding problems   235
    Close and follow-up   236
    Summary   238

13 Conclusions: the mindset and myths of influence   **241**

The mindset of influence   244

Learning the art of influence   249

Influence: the one sin and four myths   250

Introduction

The art of influence

From the age of deference to the age of influence

Thirty years ago a revolution was started with a pair of grey socks. The top executives of Procter & Gamble walked onto the platform at a company conference. As they took their seats there was a shocked silence as everyone realised that one executive had broken ranks with all the others. He was wearing dark grey socks, not black socks. There was a suspicion that he was not just being revolutionary, but also downright unpatriotic.

Thirty years later all the top executives of Skype gathered for a conference in Estonia. Everyone, including the CEO, wore the regulation uniform of jeans and T-shirt. Well, nearly everyone. I was the speaker, and felt very overdressed in casual shirt and trousers. Remarkably, attendees wore different coloured socks without a revolution breaking out. Some were even wearing tights, not because of a fetish for cross-dressing, but because they were women. Being a white middle-aged male is no longer a precondition for success.

In one generation, dress codes have changed out of all recognition, and so have the rules of survival and success. In the old order there was a clear hierarchy and the trappings of power were highly visible. It was a caste system where the highest caste people had reserved parking spaces, separate dining rooms and elevators, the biggest desks and offices and the freshest flowers and deepest carpets. It was an arrangement which was very acceptable to the people at the top.

The world of hierarchy was also a world of command and control. Workers worked and bosses bossed: workers had the hands and bosses had the brains. Workers were expected to do what they were told. At its best, it was a paternalistic world where firms and governments looked after workers and voters. At worst, it was a recipe for strikes, strife and conflict between the haves and the have-nots.

The old world is passing away. Black socks are not mandatory and respect for the hierarchy is evaporating. Public trust in politicians, business leaders, journalists, union leaders and lawyers is at an all-time low in opinion polls in both the USA and UK. The self-styled elites may still believe in themselves, but no one else does. We are more likely to trust a favourite band or a favourite brand than we are to trust the men in suits.

Even within organisations, old-style command and control is breaking down. The world of compliance is giving way to the world of commitment: you cannot order people to be committed. You have to build commitment over time. And commitment, unlike control, is a two-way street.

The old world of command and control enabled and imprisoned people at the same time. Power and position used to march hand in hand. Success meant slowly climbing the career ladder. Power grew with position, but was limited by position. This was an acceptable formula for patient people who were happy to climb the career ladder for 30 years before gaining a position of power, prestige and influence. That is a formula which is deeply unattractive to anyone entering the workforce today. Thirty years ago, at the start of the grey socks revolution, Freddie Mercury of Queen sang 'I want it all and I want it now.' It was revolutionary rock. The difference today is that people want more and they want it faster.

> command and control enabled and imprisoned people

Just as individuals want to break free from the limitations of command and control, so organisations need people who can move beyond command and control. Command and control structures were typically functional silos. Today, organisations are flatter and more fragmented. It is easy to hide but hard to shine in such complex organisations. It is even harder to make things happen. In flat organisations you cannot boss people around so much because you may not control them: they work in different functions or even in different companies. Instead of using authority, you have to use influence: creating coalitions, building willing followers, picking the right agenda, fostering networks of trust and support. This is not just a different skill set from command and control, it is a different mindset.

The age of influence opens up huge opportunities. It removes our dependence on hierarchy. By building our own networks and platforms for success we can make things happen, fulfil our dreams and achieve our ambitions. We can control our own fate. To do this, we have to learn a whole new art: the art of influence.

The invisible hand of influence

Where the trappings of power are visible, the skills of influence are invisible. We can see that some people have influence. It is much less obvious how they gained and use influence. The signs of an influential person are plain to see: they have a web of willing allies; they seem to be in the right place at the right time; they turn crises into conflict and turn opposition into support. Lack of control does not lead to lack of progress: their network enables them to achieve much more than the lone hero trying to do it all alone.

At first, influence appears to be one of those mysterious qualities like charisma or inspiration: you either have it or you do not. Fortunately, this is not the case. Effective influencers display some consistent skills and behaviours which anyone can learn. Behind those behaviours is a mindset: that is the invisible key to influence. We cannot see what people think. But if we understand how they think, then we can start to use the same way of thinking and achieve the same results. The influencer's way of thinking differs from normal thinking in many ways, for instance:

- Prefers trust to friendship and allies to friends
- Sees the world through others' eyes, not just their own
- Offers measured generosity: neither selfishness nor complete selflessness.
- Has ambition, but not just for themselves.
- Starts at the end and focuses on outcomes: not first things first
- Can be ruthless and unreasonable, but not unfair.

In total, *How to Influence* maps out over 60 skills, principles and behaviours which influential people consistently use. Each skill is based on observed practice. This is not a theory of influence: it is practice as it happens in the real world. Because the book is practice-based, each skill is supported by real examples, stories or cases. The book is not a course: it does not attempt to provide a detailed recipe for deploying each skill. Instead, it maps out the main principles which influencers follow. In reality, each influencer has their own style: they focus on some skills more than others and use them in different ways. Armed with the principles of influence you can decide which skills to develop and how to deploy them. You do not have to become someone else to be an effective influencer. You simply build on the best of who you already are.

Influence versus persuasion

Influence is not the same as persuasion. Influencers play for much higher stakes than persuaders. Persuasion is the art of convincing someone to buy something or do something once. There are plenty of tricks and tactics for achieving a one-off success. But such success is not just short-lived: it can destroy longer-term influence. If I have been persuaded to do something once, against my better judgement, then I will be twice as careful and resistant next time the persuader comes calling with another idea. Successful persuasion can work once and prevent further success.

Influencers do not want a one-off success. They want to build commitment which lasts. This means that influencers think and act very differently from persuaders. Persuaders start and finish with their own needs. They want to sell their product or plant their idea in another person's head. Communication tends to be one-way: the persuader does most of the talking as they extol the virtues of the product or idea they want to push.

Influencers still have goals to achieve, but think differently about how to get there. They see the world through other people's eyes, and adapt their message and behaviour accordingly. The ideal outcome is not simply to persuade someone: it is to build an alliance of mutual trust and respect. Achieving this is a huge investment of time, effort and skill. But it is an investment which yields rich dividends over a long period.

The journey towards influence

> The things we really need to know and learn to succeed are not taught

The things we really need to know and learn to succeed are not taught. We have to pick them up from experience. But the random walk of experience can be very painful: it is full of dead ends, booby traps, cliff edges and endless swamps. *How to Influence* puts some structure into that random walk. The book is based on 30 years of research, observation and work with nearly 100 of the best, and one or two of the worst, organisations on our planet. They have covered every main industry sector as well as public and voluntary sectors in Asia, Europe and North America. The good news is that influence is a universal skill with consistent behaviour patterns which anyone can learn. We can take some of the randomness out of our random walk of experience: that means we can learn faster and progress faster.

> the random walk of experience can be very painful

Inevitably, influence and power can be put to good use or bad use. I hope you use influence to be a force for good, but this book does not try to be moral or immoral. Its only purpose is to show how you can acquire power and influence: how you use it is up to you and your conscience.

This book not only shows you how to build influence: it also helps you resist unwelcome attempts to influence or manipulate you. Once you have learned the patterns and principles of influence, you are better equipped to spot them and resist them. The best influencing techniques are largely invisible: that is what makes them so effective and dangerous. Unless you know what you are looking for, you will not even realise you are being influenced. Once you recognise the pattern, you can make a decision to resist or cooperate: at least you will have a choice which many of your colleagues will not even realise that they have.

As you embark on your journey of influence, you will make a pleasant discovery: influence is self-reinforcing. The more influential you become, the easier it is to acquire even more influence. More and more people will want to work with you as you build up your influence. Influence enables you to do more, fix things, strike deals and make things happen. Everyone will want some of your pixie dust, and will

> influence is self-reinforcing

be more than happy to reciprocate in any way they can. The challenge is to move from being an outsider to being the centre of the network. Life on the outside of the network is lonely, frustrating and hard work. *How to Influence* shows how you can make the journey from outsider to the centre of influence.

With over 60 influencing skills and principles to absorb, no one can hope to start at page one and finish at the end as the complete influencer. Instead, use this book as a reference guide. Focus on one skill at a time. Experiment and practise. Find your own style of deploying these skills. Influencing is not about working from some mechanical script. It is about using a range of skills to build voluntary and lasting support from the people you influence. Apply the skills in ways that are natural to you.

The best influencers make their skills invisible. No one realises they are being persuaded or influenced. They simply find it very easy to support and work with the influencer, without being sure why they find it so easy. When you can make the invisible hand of influence work for you, then you have truly mastered the art. *How to Influence* makes those invisible skills visible for you.

Part One

The art of influence:
acquiring influence
and authority

Chapter 1

Build your platform

was Mr Zest and in the next cubicle sat Mr Fairy. I was responsible for Zest (a toilet soap). He was responsible for a competitor: Fairy toilet soap. On balance, I preferred to be Mr Zest rather than Mr Fairy. Suddenly, the CEO appeared by our cubicles: he was on walkabout. He asked me how things were going. I muttered something about the weather. He moved on to Mr Fairy and asked the same question.

'Jurgen,' said Mr Fairy, 'I would really like your advice on this new promotion we are developing. . .' The CEO was delighted. This was his chance to show that he had lost none of his marketing skills. Fifteen minutes later Jurgen left with a big smile on his face: he had just proven he still had the right stuff. Mr Fairy also had a big smile. He had just got the CEO's support for a controversial new promotion, and had made his name with the big boss. Word quickly spread that the Fairy project was now the CEO's pet project. One week later, all the staff departments had waved Fairy's promotion through. One month later, I was still battling with them to gain approval for my far more modest promotion.

In that short exchange with the CEO, Mr Fairy had demonstrated several key influencing techniques:

- He seized the moment
- He sold his idea by asking for advice: he listened rather than pitching

- He had acted as a partner to the boss, treating him as a human not just a boss.
- He borrowed the authority of the CEO.

The easiest way for people without influence (like Mr Zest and Mr Fairy) to gain influence is to borrow it from someone else. The power of endorsement from the right people is huge. Advertisers understand this well. Makers of sportswear, like Nike and Adidas, relentlessly pursue endorsements from the top sports stars of the day in each sport. As consumers we know that the stars have been bought: they may or may not prefer Adidas or Nike. But still the endorsement works. We like to believe that if we have the same gear as the champions we can play as well as them, or at least better than we normally do. In truth, the clubs which Tiger Woods uses may need more control than an amateur can achieve: we might be better off with clubs which are more forgiving of error. But such is the power of endorsement, we will pay a premium for the gear which our sporting heroes advocate.

Influential people do not have to rely on office and status for power. They create their own form of informal power. They all have a platform which they cultivate carefully. These platforms represent a short cut to power and influence. Instead of waiting and hoping for promotion, these platforms offer influence and power in a hurry.

There are four main types of platform for the influential manager:

- Influential people: borrow credibility and influence
- Influential places: go where the power is
- Claims to fame: build your personal platform
- Agenda control: have a plan.

It is possible to grow all four sorts of influence at the same time. Influential people and places are about borrowing a platform for influence. They are short cuts to influence. At some point managers also need to acquire influence in their own right. Agenda control and having a claim to fame give managers a personal platform of influence.

Influential people: borrow credibility and influence

We can borrow money for the short term, perhaps on our credit cards, and we can borrow money for the long term, perhaps on our mortgage. In the same way, managers can borrow influence in both the short term and the long term. In the short term, borrowed influence comes from the power of endorsements. Long-term borrowing of power comes from patronage: making alliances with the right power barons. Both sorts of borrowing increase the influence which a manager can exert in an organisation.

Short-term borrowing: the power of endorsement

The power of endorsement became clear when I found myself at Lloyds, the reinsurance underwriting business. I had imagined it would be a highly sophisticated and complicated business underwriting the risk of oil rigs, supertankers, aircraft and football stars' feet. I was wrong. The broker went round various old-fashioned desks where underwriters sat. The broker pulled out a piece of paper with a $3 billion risk on a North Sea oil rig. The underwriter looked at the piece of paper. 'OK,' he said after about ten seconds, 'If it's good enough for Charlie, Tom and Jamie its good enough for me. I'll take a $50 million line.' He had just committed his firm to $50 million of risk on the basis that people he trusted had also taken up some of the risk. Some time later Lloyds was submerged in bad risks and nearly went bust: assessing risk on the basis of which of your friends have signed up was perhaps not smart enough.

Effective managers learn to use the power of endorsement to their advantage. Business plans, promotions and new ideas are not judged just on the basis of the idea. They are also judged on the quality of the people behind the idea. In the same way, venture capitalists do not judge a new business idea just on the basis of a business plan. They back the manager as much as they back the plan. There is good reason for this. A good team will improve an average plan and will make molehills out of mountains. The 'B' team will struggle to live up to its promises. Until you have an established track record, you will be regarded as the 'B' team: you will be judged on performance, not on potential.

Long-term borrowing of power: the power of patronage

When Kensington Palace was first built it gave great amusement to the peasants of Kensington. They would gather outside and watch the high-and-mighty lords and ladies arriving in their extravagant court dress. It was like watching film stars arriving for a première, but without the respect and adulation which film stars receive. For their part, the lords and ladies would carry nosegays of perfumed herbs to protect their very refined noses from the smells of the great unwashed: in practice, however, even the lords and ladies stank. They would change their outer clothes several times a day, and they would change their underclothes three or four times a year. Everyone wanted to petition the king, but access was limited. Some people would wait for days in one of the many waiting rooms and antechambers. The smarter petitioners would seek the patronage of aristocrats who already had access to the king. Power and money flowed from the king: the closer you were, the more influence, power and prestige you had.

The kings of the corporate world are CEOs. Hopefully, they change their underwear more often than the kings of the past. But still power and patronage flows from the CEO, and still the power barons gather round their corporate king, jostling for position and for favours. Those who do well can, like Cardinal Richelieu under Louis XIII, find fame and fortune. Those who displease the king suffer corporate execution: they are fired.

The principles of patronage apply as much in the corporate world as they did in the era of powerful kings and queens. Access to the top is desirable, but for many managers access to a power baron is a very useful substitute. Picking the right power baron is not easy. The right power baron has two qualities:

- *Success*: they will have or acquire significant patronage in terms of bonuses, pay, promotions, projects and assignments.
- *Loyalty*: they will stick with and reward the team that helped them succeed.

Patronage is a two-way street: the patron always wants something in return for what they give. The stronger the give and take, the deeper the loyalty and commitment is likely to be. Michael demonstrated how to be a power baron when he started a new service line offering post-merger integration support to clients. First, he was successful: he built the business rapidly. That gave him a pot of bonus money and influence over promotions which made him a highly attractive power. Second, he was fiercely loyal to his team and demanded 100 per cent loyalty in return. His team became like a firm within a firm. Outsiders were not welcome and it became very hard to judge who was doing what inside the team. Only Michael really knew what was going on. He used success and knowledge to his advantage. At promotion time he backed his three candidates vigorously. Michael essentially bullied the promotion commission into accepting his picks: the only perform-ance benchmark the commission had came from Michael, who was clearly successful. Success and loyalty breeds dedicated followers. They also attract some of the best and most ambitious talent into his team.

Michael expects his pound of flesh in return. Total loyalty and total commitment are required. His team is like a cult: it has its own values, beliefs and ways of doing things. They are not just loyal to Michael: they are loyal to each other.

If surrendering your ego, life and career to that of an emerging power baron is a step too far, there are other weaker but still effective forms of patronage which managers can cultivate. A good mentoring relationship can be highly productive for both sides: as with all forms of patronage it should be a win–win relationship. This is what each side should expect:

- *Mentee*: gains access to a senior executive. Personal advice and support helps; an insight into how senior managers think is invaluable preparation for dealing with other senior managers; the mentor should also alert the mentee to emerging career opportunities and risks, and should be able to help break the occasional political logjam. The mentor may not give much time, but the value of each intervention can be huge.

- *Mentor*: the mentor values having eyes and ears across the organisation. Top executives distrust formal papers which are submitted to them: such papers give a warped version of the truth. They value word of mouth about what is really going on across the organisation. They also need some 'go-to' people for discretionary help and support on building a new idea, making a speech or preparing a meeting. Finally, most mentors are quietly flattered that emerging talent is seeking them out and values their views.

The main block to forming such relationships is normally in the mentee's head. We look at the big bosses and think of them as big bosses. We let the hierarchy get in the way of the relationship. As we shall see in the chapter on the Partnership Principle, the trick is to remember that even the biggest boss is still a human being, despite appearances to the contrary. If we treat them as humans and partners, not just as bosses, we are more likely to establish a productive relationship with them.

Influential places: go where the power is

Willy Sutton, the famous American bank robber, was asked why he robbed banks. 'Because that is where the money is,' he replied. If you want money, go where the money is. If you want fame, go where the fame is. If you want power, go where the power is.

Some people are attracted to power like moths to a light. Inevitably, some get burned in the process. The brightest source of power and influence is the organisation you represent. A few people become influential in their own right: pop stars, actors, artists and sportspeople can all achieve influence on their own. Some, like Bono, have presidents and prime ministers jostling to get their photo taken with them. Unless we are confident of becoming a global megastar in our own right, we need a short cut to achieving position and influence. As soon as we represent an organisation, we inherit the influence and credibility of that organisation. If we join the right part of that organisation, we multiply our influence even further.

Choice of employer

When businesspeople meet in Japan, the first thing they do is exchange *meishi*, business cards. To the Western eye, meishi states someone's name, employer and position. In practice, meishi are guides to who should have bowed first, longest and deepest upon introduction. The person's title and company will indicate their status: Toyota is clearly more prestigious than one of its suppliers or the local corner shop. As the meishi are read and exchanged, vigorous bowing ensues to

> meishi are guides to who should have bowed first, longest and deepest

establish the right social order. Bowing may seem difficult to Westerners, but try explaining how to shake hands to a Japanese businessman (when, how do you know it is time, how do you show you want to shake hands, how hard, how long?).

The tale of the meishi shows how far we depend on our employer for our status and influence. If you work for McKinsey, executives are likely to answer the phone when you call. If you are calling from Fred's Consulting Emporium, you will find it much harder to contact the CEO you wished to talk to. Every time we call, every time we state our employer's name, we borrow all their credibility: we inherit the influence and power built up over years by the firm. To see the power of the employer, watch what happens to senior executives when they leave the big firms they used to run. The masters of the universe become outcasts: no one takes their call. Even CEOs become shadows of themselves once they step down.

Choosing the right firm is fundamental to influence. Choosing a large and prestigious firm is a short cut to personal prestige and influence in the marketplace. This is reflected in the recruiting season at undergraduate and graduate levels: the top employers in consulting, law and banking are inundated with applications from the best and the brightest. They are like the moths attracted to the light. They all fervently believe that they are better and brighter than the rest of the best and the brightest. Slowly, they discover the relentless logic of the career pyramid. If there is one partner for every 25 employees, then even with 10 per cent growth a year, just one in ten of the graduates will make partner inside ten years. Nine out of ten will be disappointed, or will come up with elaborate reasons around how they had always really wanted to start a vegan farm in Vermont. That puts the challenge of influence and power into perspective. If you join the large and prestigious firm, you will need to do more than be bright and work hard to succeed. The art of influence becomes essential: to stand out, to make things happen, to have a claim to fame and to find the right assignments and opportunities in order to succeed.

not all nations are equal in a global firm

Global firms would appear at first glance to give the widest range of opportunities. To some extent, they do.

But global firms are rarely global: not all nations are equal in a global firm. In global firms, the influential place is the home nation. French, Japanese, American, Indian and Chinese firms may hire plenty of foreigners. Some may be promoted to senior positions. But the overwhelming weight of power is with the home-country nationals. This is routinely reflected in the choice of CEO, who normally comes from the home nation. Exceptions, such as Carlos Ghosn (Nissan) or Howard Stringer (Sony) are notable precisely because they are exceptions to the rule.

Home-country bias also causes serious problems lower in the organisation. Global teams rarely work as well as they are meant to. Part of the problem is about power. As one Welsh worker with a French company explained: 'I never see the team leader: all the decisions seem to be made over there. I try double guessing what is expected but it is a waste of time. They don't trust us and we don't trust them.' The place of power is clear: it is nearly always with the home nation. Choose your employer well.

Choice of function

As this book went to press, Procter & Gamble announced that Robert McDonald was taking over from A.G. Lafley as the new CEO. I did not have to guess what his background was. I knew what his background had to be. The only source of power and influence at P&G is marketing and brand management. He had to have come from that route. A quick check showed that this was the case. His marketing career had taken him from North America to Japan and Asia, giving him the global outlook which P&G wanted from the new CEO. The only way to the top at P&G is through brand management. Even at the lowest levels of the firm, this truism is keenly felt: it is the brand groups which drive most of the critical business decisions across the firm on a day-to-day basis. Manufacturing, sales, R&D, finance, logistics and HR all have vital roles to play. But it is clear that the brands are in the driving seat. If you want power and influence at P&G, joining brand management is a smart move. True to the rule of home country bias, both A.G. Lafley and McDonald are US citizens: P&G may be global, but it is clear where power lies: in America and in marketing.

In many other firms, the choice of function is not so clear-cut. In professional service firms, the nature of power and influence is constantly shifting in response to the market: one industry group or service line will grow rapidly and another shrink. The managers in the growing business all look like heroes; the managers in the shrinking businesses get to wear the dunce's cap. Power follows the money and money follows the client: if cash is king then the client is the emperor. The ideal place to be is in a small business unit which is about to grow rapidly. This is much easier said than done.

Claims to fame

Old Uncle Harry had a good war. As he recounted his various tales of the war it became clear that he had, single-handed, defeated Nazism (with perhaps a little help from the Russians, Americans and that nice Mr Churchill). The truth was a little more mundane: he had been in the supply corps and never got too close to the action. But that was never going to stop him telling a good tale or two. Harry's claim to fame lasted to his dying day and had served him very well by impressing prospective employers and girlfriends.

A good claim to fame can make a person or an organisation. Tom Peters is a superstar on the corporate speaking circuit. His original claim to fame was to have been a co-author of *In Search Of Excellence*. That is now a widely unread book which languishes in the lower reaches of the Amazon rankings. Even though the original platform is past its sell-by date, it has served its purpose: it has given Tom Peters the chance to build his speaking career.

Similarly, Microsoft benefits from a success platform which has now disappeared. When IBM entered the PC market it was the dominant force in mainframes. It was expected to set the standard in the PC market as well. It happened to choose a start-up run by Bill Gates to provide the operating system for its computer. The result is that Microsoft became the de facto standard operating system for all PCs. IBM exited the PC business in 2005 when it completed the sale of its PC division to Lenovo. Microsoft's original platform disappeared, but it still retains a 90 per cent share of the market for desktop operating systems. The mystery of a good platform is that it works even after it has disappeared.

> The mystery of a good platform is that it works even after it has disappeared

Most of us are not going to publish a best-seller, become a corporate speaking superstar or grab 90 per cent of a global market. But we still need our claim to fame if we are to make our mark. The need for a claim to fame is becoming more important as organisations become flatter and more confusing. One life insurance company manages to have five dimensions to its matrix: products, channels, geographies, customers and functions. Most human beings struggle with more than three dimensions. Even actuaries struggle with five. In complex firms it is easy to hide and even harder to shine. No one knows who was really responsible for what. This matters. If you are just another grey face in cubicle land, it is hard to have influence or power. If you have a claim to fame, you get noticed more and you find more opportunities come your way.

> In complex firms it is easy to hide and even harder to shine

The power of the claim to fame became clear at promotion time. I was tasked with running the promotions commission. There were 30 promotions to hand out among 50 nominees: officially we were told there was no limit. Never trust company propaganda. This meant that there were going to be 20 desperately disappointed people. Firing people is relatively easy: by the time it gets to that stage, both sides recognise the inevitable. Disappointing good people who have worked hard and achieved much is far worse. We sifted through the promotions packages. They were all eulogies of unstinting praise to the extraordinary success of each individual. They were, in other words, a pack of lies. Each pack was an attempt by a boss to fulfil a promise made to a team member: 'work hard and I will get you promoted.'

In the end, we had to ask ourselves three questions:

- Who is sponsoring the candidate? (are the sponsors credible and trustworthy?)
- What is our personal experience of the candidate?
- What is the candidate's claim to fame?

The sponsorship question leads back to the influential people principle: you need a powerful sponsor. The personal experience question leads back to the influential places question: it is much easier to make a positive impression if you work in proximity to the people who will decide your career. It is also possible to make a negative impression more easily. The final question was the decider: what was the candidate's claim to fame?

A claim to fame could be more or less anything. One person had become the company expert in the arcane art of building financial business cases for IT projects in UK life assurance companies. It was arcane, but valuable. He got promoted. Another person was notable because she always volunteered to help out with discretionary effort, and she always delivered. She got promoted. Another had been sent to Cumbria on a small, messy project and had turned it into a large and successful project. He got promoted.

The claim to fame principle can send you into voluntary exile. If it is hard to stand out in cubicle land, it is easier to stand out in the outposts of empire where you have the chance to run your own show. You can be a big fish in a small pond and learn how big fish behave. Running your own show means that failure or success is very clearly owned by you. If you decide to do this, there are two golden rules to remember:

- Never believe any promises about what will happen on your return from exile
- Manage your reputation at head office vigorously.

These are lessons I learned the hard way when I decided to take voluntary exile and run a business in Japan. When I arrived I found a business with no customers, no sales, no prospect of any sales and a lot of bills to pay. My one-way ticket to Japan appeared to be a one-way ticket to career hospice. Looked at more positively, if I did anything it would be an improvement on the mess I inherited. So I bought a series of round-the-world tickets in both directions and started to manage expectations in our two head offices, based inconveniently in New Jersey and Paris. The key was to make sure that our story about Japan was the accepted story: we quickly constructed a story about investment. We could either invest in Japan for three years and build a business which fitted with the rest of the world, or we could close down and exit, or we could throw the dice and buy another company at huge cost. If we had let the finance people construct the story, it would have been very unpleasant. By striking early, setting the tone of the debate and then finding as many excuses as possible to go back to the seat of power, we were able to survive.

Once you are in an outpost, nobody really knows or understands how well you are doing. They see the numbers and they pass judgement on that basis. That is why it is essential to manage the story behind the numbers: show that what you are doing is a real achievement and a step-change from the past.

The second lesson is never believe any promises about what will happen on your return from exile. After three years, the firm will probably have been reorganised three times and all your old line managers will be in different posts. Your new line managers will see no great need to keep old promises made by someone else to someone they do not know. And there will probably be no openings available anyway. The only antidote to this is to keep in close contact with head office during your exile. Manage the politics and keep your radar tuned in to new positions opening up.

If you survive all this, you will have a real claim to fame. You will have shown you can run something and you will stand out from all the other functionaries who analyse, report, and associate themselves with success while distancing themselves from problems. As your claims to fame build, you create a unbridgeable gap versus more cautious colleagues who have never taken the risk and never led.

Agenda control

People are busy. We seem more stressed and stretched than ever. Every day there are more challenges and crises to deal with. We need to respond to customers, competitors, colleagues and top managers. The last thing we all need is the chance to do more: we already have too much to do, thank you very much.

The problem of stress and overwork is a wonderful opportunity for influential managers. There are countless opportunities to quietly take control: most people will be delighted that you are taking a problem away from them. They are not just giving you a problem; they are giving you an opportunity to build your influence. Controlling the agenda is a powerful platform from which you can grow your influence.

Taking control gracefully, as opposed to having a power battle, is based on three requirements:

- Find the right opportunity
- Strike early
- Move centre stage.

I discovered all three of these rules by accident as a young researcher in the British Parliament. My boss was an MP and responsible for economic and industrial policy. He decided the party needed a new economic and industrial policy. This was not strictly true. The party did not need a new policy: he needed a new policy to show that he was doing something. So he assembled a group of very important people to advise him. They all sat round a table and pontificated for an hour or two. I was gently ignored: I was far too young to be capable of thinking or speaking. Towards the end of the meeting, I made the only contribution I could: I offered to summarise the meeting for them. They were delighted: that was an administrative chore which was beneath their dignity. I did not realise it at the time, but a well-chosen administrative chore can be an administrative coup.

> a well-chosen administrative chore can be an administrative coup

Back at the office, I looked at my scrawled notes. All the grand people had said grand things, but there was no conclusion or direction to any of the comments. So I wrote what I thought would be a good industrial and economic policy, taking care to include one or two comments from each grandee. I then circulated the summary, drawing each recipient's attention to their contribution. They were delighted to see that one of their ideas was getting into the policy document. A couple of revisions later, the policy was agreed. It was, by accident, my policy. Two years later, the whole party imploded: I like to think that it was not my fault.

Let's call up the slow-motion replay and see what happened:

- *Find the right opportunity.* Working on the party's economic and industrial policy was better than responding to constituents' housing worries.

- *Strike early.* There are always moments of uncertainty when it is not clear who is going to do what. There is a void waiting to be filled, so fill it. Someone needs to step up and volunteer to solve the problem, lead the analysis, summarise the meeting or take the next steps. The first person to raise their hands, cough, catch the eye of the chairperson or even raise an eyebrow is the person who volunteers. Normally, everyone else will be delighted that they have dodged extra work.

- *Move centre stage.* Offering to facilitate, take notes or summarise sounds tedious and a bit like hard work. It is. But it also puts you centre stage. The facilitator controls the direction of the conversation; the summariser controls the output of the meeting. Anyone can do this at any level.

Taking notes is not the only way to take control. There are always tasks which no one else wants to do; they are too busy and the task is too difficult. That is the void waiting to be filled. Most times, it makes sense to leave the void well alone. If it is a low-value task, you simply add to an overcrowded agenda. If it is an opportunity which gives you the chance to shine, strike early and volunteer. Two examples will make the point:

We were setting up a charity. There was a huge amount to do: fundraising, finding staff, building our operations. Fortunately, a kind businessman volunteered to do the tedious work of liaising with lawyers and charity commission to set up the legal structure. It was bureaucracy we were pleased to delegate. And at that moment we lost control of the charity. He used the legal process to install himself as chairman and his friends as trustees. Once installed, there was no way of removing them. They were useless and nearly killed the charity. He filled the void and took control.

The second example took place in a dire company meeting, the sort which all executives have to endure from time to time. Budgets for the following year were being agreed. Head office staff were like rottweilers. They attacked every increase in spending from the operating units. Finally, they got up and announced an increase of 40 per cent, or $35 million in their own head office budget. There was stunned silence. At the first objection, the COO smiled thinly. 'Well,' he said, 'if anyone thinks we can spend less, they are welcome to come to head office and prove it to us.' No one was foolish enough to take on the power and might of head office: that is a death wish. Well, nearly no one. There is always one person with more courage than sense. I raised my hand. The void had been filled and I had volunteered for the death wish project of cutting head office budget and making enemies of every power broker in the company. Be careful which opportunities you take on.

Summary

There are four main ways of building a power base for the influential manager:

- Borrow power: influential people
- Go where the power is: influential places
- Build your reputation: have a claim to fame
- Control the agenda: have a plan.

All of this amounts to a BFO: a blinding flash of the obvious. Like much of the art of management it is not a deep secret known only to a few wizards of the art. It is common sense: common sense is in short supply in many workplaces. If you can apply these principles you will already start to acquire influence. As ever, applying common sense in the messy, ambiguous, shifting world of management is not easy. This chapter has described what the influential manager needs to build influence. The following chapters will show how to build these power bases and how to build influence. But first, we will explore further the principle of influential people: knowing who to influence and how to weave your web of influence across your organisation.

common sense is in short supply in many workplaces

Chapter 2

Create a network

The first day at work, like the first day at school, can be traumatic. You want to make a good impression, but you don't know anyone and have no idea what to do or how things work. The trauma remains even if you join at a senior level, as I found out when I joined a large firm as a partner.

I arrived on my first day. No one knew me: even the receptionist looked at me blankly and said that no one of my name worked there. Good start. I then enjoyed the ritual humiliation of having to be told how the phones and computers worked: I could not even make a phone call or send an email without help. So much for being a master of the universe. I was shown into a big office. My office. I sat in the big chair behind the big desk. Reality set in fast: with no clients and no team I had no prospects. I needed to make things happen. But even if I could get the phone to work: who to call and what to call them about?

It was a stark contrast to my previous place: I knew everyone and had a stable of clients. If I needed to make anything happen, I knew who to call for what. I also knew who to avoid. I had two networks of influence in my old organisation. Internally I had a network of alliances and mutual obligations which I could call on. Externally, I had a network of clients who provided revenues and work. Suddenly, I was without all the networks that made success possible. I was the proverbial fish out of water. I discovered too late the advice about all headhunters: when headhunters promise greener pastures elsewhere, remember, it's greenest where it rains the most.

> when headhunters promise greener pastures elsewhere, remember, it's greenest where it rains the most

To succeed, I needed to start weaving new webs of influence inside and outside the firm. This is the challenge all managers face. Influence comes from having a network of alliances and trust: people you can call on to make things happen. Networks of influence enjoy the benefits and challenges of the network effect: strong networks get stronger, weak networks stay weak.

The network effect is pervasive in business. A telephone system with just one line has limited use: the more people join the network, the more attractive it becomes. Many web businesses enjoy the benefits of the network effect. eBay is attractive to sellers because it attracts so many buyers and vice versa: the more customers it has, the more attractive it becomes. It has liquidity and depth which other online markets cannot match. In financial markets, the largest stock exchanges and other financial markets enjoy the same network advantages of scale and liquidity for buyers and sellers.

In the management world, the network effect drives influence. A manager with no network has no influence; worse, he is unlikely to attract any alliances or support. He has little to offer in return. A well-networked manager attracts talent and attracts more alliances. The well-networked manager can do deals, return favours, provide access to key people, work the politics and make things happen. The strong network attracts and the weak network repels.

> The strong network attracts and the weak network repels

The purpose of this chapter is only to show what sort of network managers need. There is no point in building up a huge quick-dial list on your mobile phone if you have the wrong people on the list. A large network is not much use if it is the wrong network. The key is to target the right people. This chapter answers the question: 'who are the right people for my network?' Subsequent chapters will show how you can attract these people into your web and make them willing allies.

It takes time and effort to build this power web, so it pays to build the right web with the right people. If the spider weaves its web in the wrong place, it will be a very hungry spider.

Weaving the right web of influence

Essentially, there are four sorts of people the influencer needs in a power web.

- *Power barons*: these are typically more senior people who have access to money and resources. They are also essential for helping with the politics. They can guide you to the right projects; they can help you get started with the right mandate, right support and right budget; they can help unblock resistance when it inevitably occurs.

- *Technocrats*. These people often live in staff functions. They cannot make things happen, but they can stop things happening. Technocrats have the power of 'no'. Even worse, they have the power to comment and advise. They can analyse and advise your project to death. Their natural habitat is in places like Finance, HR, Legal, Health and Safety and even the brand police.

- *Resources*: these are team members who will work directly for you. Typically you will be offered a mix of the new and the struggling, on the basis that they are the only people available. The 'B' team is a recipe for long nights, high anxiety and even higher stress. Influential managers will use their skills and networks to identify, woo and recruit the 'A' team.

- *Trading partners.* Traders are typically at a similar level to you. They exist in an ambiguous world of cooperation and competition with each other. They have to collaborate to make things happen, but they are competing for the same pot of budgets, management support, promotions and bonuses.

It takes time to find out where real power lies. Obviously, A CEO is powerful. But in day-to-day life other people may be more important for making things happen. For instance, Sarah worked at an advertising agency. It was full of people with loud shirts, loud mouths and huge egos. The Account Managers were all intense rivals. The greatest rivalry was for the support of the creative department. There was never enough creative talent to go round. The way to get work done was to get one of the big power barons to shout and scream long enough that your work would go to the front of the queue. Every power baron played the same game. It was like a chimpanzees' tea party, but with less order. To rationalise the process, the agency created the job of scheduler. The scheduler received work requests from all the big-ego account managers and worked out which creative teams should do the work when. Naturally, all the big egos stopped shouting at the creative teams (which was good) and started shouting at the scheduler instead (which was not so good). The scheduler quickly learned not to trust anything the big egos said: they all said every piece of work was the most important and the most urgent piece of work. Sarah realised where power now resided: not with the big ego bosses but with the mid-level manager who was the scheduler. She took time to get to know him; she built trust by being honest about her priorities. She helped the scheduler by letting him put a piece of her work back when he was faced with a genuine crisis elsewhere. After a while, Sarah found that she could get all her work done easily: her whisper counted with the scheduler for more than all the shouting of the big egos. She saw where the real power resided and used her influence to put that power at her disposal.

To build your own power web, you need to take stock of what you have at the moment and compare it with what you need. Start by noting whose help and support you need on your current assignment. The shape of your web will change from assignment to assignment: different people become important at different times. Over a few years, it becomes clear who is consistently important and reliable for you. The simplest starting point is to focus on your current assignment. Map out where your key relationships lie on the grid below. The basic trade-off is between power and trust: in the perfect network, all the key relationships live in the north-east quadrant of high power and high trust. Corporate life is rarely that simple, as we shall see.

One example will show the power and peril of the power web. Follow the example and draw up your own power web. This will let you see how strong your position is and where you need to build further. This is a real-life example where the names have been changed to protect the innocent and not so innocent. Chris was the sales director of a large financial firm. He was performing well: sales numbers were up even in a market that was down. Despite this, he did not feel secure in his position. The first step was to map his power web, which is illustrated below.

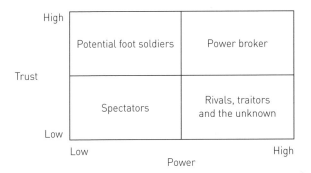

The web of influence

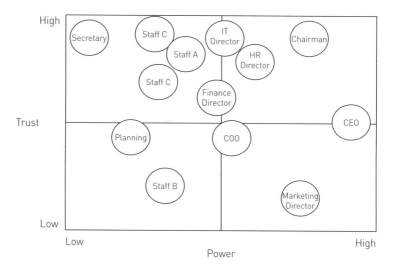

The sales director's web of influence

In practice, this was a simplified version of his power web. He had at least 40 significant relationships across the firm. He always knew who to call to get things done. Although his network was very wide, first impressions were deceptive: his web was dangerously weak.

The most glaring problem was with his boss: the CEO. The one person we all need to have the greatest bond of trust with is also the most powerful person in our work: our boss. Chris had, at best, a mixed relationship with the boss. Occasional periods of calm would be interrupted by violent storms of disagreement, which could be followed by a tense sulk on both sides. Their behaviour was childish, which is not uncommon in the executive suite. Chris also had a violent relationship with the Marketing Director. They were at each other's throats. Marketing would always blame Sales and Sales would always blame Marketing for any setbacks. The salespeople blamed marketing for poorly designed and overpriced products which arrived too late. Marketing saw Sales as a bunch of overpaid, lazy, incompetent whingers. It was a divisive relationship that invited the rest of the executive team to take sides. Most of the rest of the team tried to stay aloof: IT, HR and Finance all claimed to have good relations with both Marketing and Sales. At least, that is what they said in public. Chris had no idea what they thought in private or what they whispered to the CEO.

Chris's biggest ally was the Chairman, which was good except that the Chairman was one year away from retirement. Power was visibly slipping away from him. Chris also thought he had good support from his direct reports: that is a delusion that all bosses have. They are the last to hear what their staff really think of them. Looking more widely, there were one or two other minor problems. The staff in the Planning department were unhelpful. Chris dismissed them as acolytes of Marketing and thought they were not powerful. He did not know how much access they had to the CEO. Because they were outside the main power structure, they appeared to be neutral and so the CEO trusted them. Chris seriously underestimated their importance.

Mapping the power web gave Chris a wake-up call. It showed that it was not enough to rely on doing a good job selling in the market. He needed to start managing the politics and the people much better. As with many executives, he was not truly aware of the politics: how he was perceived and who had influence over whom. He needed a reality check. He was working against the organisation, not with it most of the time. This explained why he was feeling such stress in his role.

At about this time, Chris got a call from a headhunter who offered him an exciting job elsewhere. Switching employer can be very dangerous for two reasons:

● The culture may be different with different rules of survival and success. New employer and employee often clash and eventually part ways as a result.

- The new employee has a very weak power web: they do not have a network of influence and trust to call on. They do not know how to make things happen, what levers to pull. They go from being a power broker in their old firm to being an outsider in the new firm. They highly effective manager suddenly appears ineffective because they cannot make things happen, they do not understand the politics.

Despite this, Chris decided to move. He would get much more salary and much less politics, he hoped. We looked at his power web when he arrived, and it is shown in full below:

It shows the challenge of all job hoppers. You start off in a very weak position knowing very few people. In this case he had a big sponsor in the CEO, but everyone else was fairly neutral because they did not really know him. He took his PA with him from his previous job, so at least she was a supporter. The good news with starting with a blank sheet of paper is that you can recreate your own personality: you can define yourself how you want to be defined. But you have to start making that reputation and building the power web very fast.

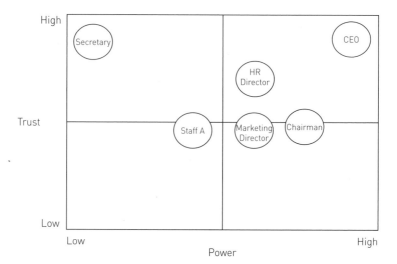

The sales director's web of influence – in his new firm

As you build your own power web, be wary of two common traps.

- *Power*: it is easy to rely too much on one or two people to sponsor us through an organisation. That makes us dependent and weak: if our sponsor moves internally or to another firm, we will find ourselves in trouble. And it is also easy to overlook people who have more power than their title might imply. Just because someone is not senior does not mean they lack power or influence. They might have the ear of the CEO, or perhaps they are a technocrat who can make life difficult for us.

- *Trust*: it is human nature to think well of ourselves and of how we are seen by other people. We are likely to overestimate how much colleagues trust us. They are likely to be courteous and professional to our faces. We may not hear what they really think. Ignore what they tell you: focus on how they work with you: do they play hard to get? Are they quick or slow to respond to requests for help? Do they ever reach out to you to ask or offer help and advice? How much do you know about them and their lives, and what makes them tick?

For all the people you need in your power web you should be able to complete the checklist below. The checklist does two things. First it checks how realistic your assessment of your power relationships is: the less you can fill in, the more you should doubt the strength of your relationship. Second, it provides a quick guide to what you need to know and the sorts of actions you need to take to build your relationship.

Influence checklist

Name	Hot issues
Position/title	Red flags
Phone	Last contacted
Mobile	Next steps
Style compass (see Chapter 9)	

This is a list you should be able to complete in your head. There are obvious risks attached to filling a notebook with this sort of detail. Most of the list explains itself. The few items which require some explanation are:

- *Style compass:* The style compass is outlined in Chapter 9. The idea is to identify the working style of the person you are dealing with, so you can adapt to them as needed.

- *Hot issues:* These are the priorities, opportunities and risks which are preoccupying the person. If you know what their agenda is, you can work out how to fit in with their agenda and how you may be able to help them.

- *Red flags:* These are the no-go areas. They can include pet hates of people, projects or problems. Do not fight battles if you do not need to.

- *Last contacted:* If you have not seen someone for a while, be cautious. You probably do not have a good grip on their current agenda, and the level of interpersonal trust may be superficial.

Below is a worked example which Chris developed for his CEO. I have added in italics some of the reality checks which this profile raised.

Influence checklist: Chris for his CEO

Name: Scott X

Position/title: CEO

Phone: xxxx xxx xxxx. PA: Maria

Mobile xxxxx xxxxxx

Style compass (see Chapter 9): Short-term outlook; driven by numbers; defensive; high need for detail and control. (*Is this how the CEO behaves with everyone, or just with Chris: how do other people see him? Marketing seems to get on well with CEO – why?*)

Hot issues: Making quarterly earnings; meeting clients. Keen on opera, entertaining and mixing with important and influential people. (*As the sales director, Chris knows plenty of influential people outside the firm; he should leverage this. Give the CEO what he wants, flatter his ego by giving him access to these top people.*)

Red flags: Dislikes being challenged, especially in public. Regards anything strategic as an excuse for spending more money or for explaining past failures.

Last contacted: Daily (*this is good, normally. Except in this case most of the contacts were confrontational. They needed to have some more productive conversations and social interaction to build a bit more trust.*)

Next steps: Continue regular meetings. (*These daily meetings are destructive: they just land up arguing. Chris needs to make the relationship more productive, less confrontational. He needs to build CEO awareness of the market dynamics, get him to take a more strategic view. Perhaps setting up some lunches with top clients would appeal to the CEO, would educate him about the market and change the nature of the conversation Chris has with the CEO.*)

The purpose of the influence checklist is not to produce yet another form with boxes to check. Its purpose is to clarify and challenge your thinking about your relationships with the people you need to influence. Chris's case is typical:

- There is a mismatch between how he sees the relationship and how the boss sees the relationship. He has let a poor relationship cloud his judgement.

- If there is a problem in the relationship, Chris owns the problem. If you fall out with your boss, you have the problem, not the boss.

> If you fall out with your boss, you have the problem, not the boss

- Chris's relationship with the boss is clearly different from the boss's relationship with other team members.

- The checklist does not provide automatic answers: it encourages some objective, creative thinking about how to change things. In this case, there were some simple steps he could take to shift the nature of the relationship.

Summary

Mapping your power web is no more than a stock check. It shows what you have and what you need. It is a reality check: if you are not sure where someone is on your web, be careful. It is human nature to assume that we are well regarded, highly trusted. The truth is often more mundane: while we are at the centre of our own little worlds, we may hardly figure on the radar screen of many our colleagues. Once we have our stock check in place, we can start working on how to weave our web and how to build the right alliances and partnerships, which are the focus of the next chapter.

Chapter 3

The commitment process: building incremental commitment

There is a huge difference between persuasion and influence. Persuasion encourages someone to do something once. Influence is about encouraging them to keep on doing something and to keep on supporting you. It lasts and is based on voluntary commitment. Influence is the gift that keeps on giving.

There are ways of persuading people to do something once. Charity muggers ('chuggers') can relieve you of a few dollars in the street; door-to-door salesmen persuade you to buy stuff you do not need; store salesmen can make you spend more than you intended. There are plenty of tactics for achieving such one-off success. It is hard work. It can

> Influence is the gift that keeps on giving

be even harder work to persuade the same person a second time: this time they will be more cautious. In contrast, if you have influenced someone well, they will keep on returning to you time and time again. Persuasion is a quick fix; influence is the lasting solution.

Building lasting influence requires commitment, from both sides. Here we explore how to build commitment from a cold start. The challenge is to become the trusted partner of a stranger: they do not know you, but you want their support. There are five elements to the commitment process:

- The hook
- Making commitment a two-way street
- Building a tribe: belonging, meaning and recognition
- Gaining commitment by giving control
- Public commitment, private challenge.

The hook

The hook is finding a reason why our target should meet us and talk to us at all. Within a firm, or with established clients, this is straightforward. Inside the firm there are established networks and common agendas which make it relatively easy to talk: at least you should know their email address and telephone numbers. Clients expect calls and these often follow a regular pattern. When calling new prospects, opening new markets or tracking down very senior executives the hook becomes important: they need to have a reason to reply to you and to meet you. This is perhaps the hardest part of the engagement process. It is hard because:

- We may not know what the right sort of hook is for our target
- Our target may be hard to access, behind protective secretaries
- Few of us actually enjoy cold calling.

In practice, there are a four established hooks we can reliably use:

- Personal introductions
- The problem solution offer
- The teaser
- The request: advice and contradiction.

To see how the hook works, we will look at a real example. I wanted to start a bank. That requires at least $1 billion of capital. I checked my personal bank account. I was at least $999 million short of the required capital. So I needed to find an existing bank which would act as a partner and put up $1 billion or more. That meant I needed to talk to the CEOs of some banks. Not only did I not have a billion dollars in spare change, my contacts book was completely devoid of bank CEOs. I needed a hook to get them interested.

The first step was to find some personal introductions. This is where the Kevin Bacon game is helpful. Kevin Bacon is a film star. The game proposes that no one is more than six degrees of separation away from him: the challenge is to prove it. This game was put to the test by the BBC in 2009. They gave 40 parcels to people around the world. The goal was to get the parcel to a scientist in Boston, Marc Vidal, by passing the parcel on to someone they already knew on first name terms who they thought might be closer to the scientist. From the depths of rural Kenya and elsewhere, it took on average six steps to reach Vidal. However, of the 40 packages that the BBC started with, only three made it to the final destination. That sums up the nature of targeted networking. We may only be six steps away from the person we want to meet, but knowing which six steps to take is very hard. We can expect to set out in the wrong direction more than nine times out of ten. The journey may be short, but it is not easy. Persistence is required.

The Vidal experiment was not a freak result. Microsoft examined 30 billion messages on its instant messaging service, used by 180 million people, and found that the average separation between people was 6.6 steps. The good news is that we live in a small world: if we work at it, we can find a way through to anyone we need to find.

In practice, this meant I talked to anyone and everyone about the new bank idea. If they liked the idea it was natural to then ask if they knew anyone who might be interested. I did not restrict the request to CEOs: I was happy to meet other senior bankers who could either be part of the team, or could validate the plan, or could take me one step closer to the right CEO. If they did not like the idea, then I could still ask them if they knew anyone who might advise on it. By conceding on the big request (support for the new bank) they would return the compliment by conceding on the small request (giving the names of some more people to talk to). Eventually I found my way to several CEOs.

Even with a personal introduction, it made sense to strengthen the hook with a problem solution offer. The problem solution offer is the staple of much advertising: use our product to remove stains better; our product relieves headaches faster; our computers are more lightweight and powerful. We may dislike such advertising, but it works. We have a problem (dirty clothes, headache, etc.) and the advertising offers a solution. To be really effective, the pitch should be personal. So the next step was a short letter which looked like this:

> Dear Mr xxxx
>
> I am writing on the advice of John Jones[1] who thought it might be of mutual benefit for us explore a new business proposal. We are[2] developing a corporate middle market bank[3] which can fill a gap in your portfolio between your successful SME and corporate banking businesses[4]. We expect the bank to achieve $50 million pre-tax profits within five years.[5]
>
> I represent a group of senior bankers who have been developing this proposal and can form the start-up team to bring this idea to market fast.[6]
>
> In the first instance, it will make sense for us to have an exploratory discussion[7] to see if this idea fits with your current portfolio and priorities. I will call your secretary[8] next week to arrange a suitable time to meet you.[9]
>
> Yours truly,

No hook letter is perfect, and it does not need to be. It simply needs to work. The letter above worked as a hook. The principles behind the letter also apply to a phone pitch or any other initial contact where you need to hook someone into an initial meeting. The main principles behind the hook in the letter are numbered and explained below:

1 This is the personal introduction, right up front to grab attention. The CEO knew and respected John Jones (an alias). The goal was to stop the secretary putting the letter in the waste basket immediately. Whether writing or speaking, you need to get past the first sentence. A weak first sentence leads to switch-off.

2 Note the positive verb. Not 'might' or 'hoping to' or 'thinking about'. We are doing it, the only question is who with: if you refuse, your arch-rivals may decide to be the partner instead. In truth, we were still at the hope and wish stage. Project confidence, not uncertainty.

3 Be very clear about what the idea is, so they see it is specific and they understand it.

4 Make it highly personalised to this bank; be positive about their existing portfolio, otherwise you will encourage a defensive reaction and denial.

5 Size the prize: it is worth the CEO getting out of bed for this. It is not something for a junior analyst to look into. It answers the question: why should I bother?

6 Be credible: show there is support, momentum and commitment. In truth, the senior bankers were interested but were not going to give up their day jobs until a deal was done. This answers the question: do I believe what is being said? In other sorts of pitches endorsements from bosses, clients, experts, sports stars can all work.

7 This is an easy ask: invest an hour of your time to see if you want $50 million a year. This is the first step of incremental commitment.

8 The CEO will not read this letter, the secretary will. Promise to follow up. When you follow up she will have forgotten about or ignored your letter, so be ready to resend it. Second time round she will take it seriously because she now knows you will follow up, so she will show the letter to the CEO and ask for advice. The hardest task can be getting past the switchboard to the secretary.

9 Keep it short. The more you write, the more there is for them to disagree with or dislike.

We cannot always dangle a $50 million hook in front of someone. Sometimes we cannot even offer a solution to a problem. We need to find another sort of hook. There are two more alternatives for us.

We can offer a teaser. We can share a little of what we have to offer for free. If they like what they see, they can ask for a meeting and find out more. Teasers are commonplace, for instance:

- Research firms offer a summary of findings for free; the full report comes at full price

- You can read part of a book on Amazon for free, and then decide if you want to commit to paying for the whole book

- Free product samples, test drives of cars are simple and honest ways of letting people make their minds up before making a larger commitment

- Consulting firms offer an initial diagnostic phase at low or no cost: they always find problems which, fortunately, they can solve. At a price.

There is an even easier, and often better, way of hooking people. Instead of offering them something, ask for something. The one thing people are normally happy to give is advice. By giving advice it shows that our judgement is valued and that we have some expertise and knowledge about the subject in question. By asking for advice, we flatter someone.

There are two ways of asking for advice:

- Ask for advice
- Encourage contradiction.

Ask for advice

Asking for advice is as simple as it sounds. I wanted to gain some clients in France, so I wrote to various targets saying I was doing research on Anglo-French leadership: the theory was that

> Asking for advice gently exploits the vanity of managers

France has a different and potentially better leadership model than the UK. Could I come and discuss this with them? As a teaser which reinforced my credentials, I sent an article with the summary of my findings on Anglo-Saxon leadership. The more senior the French businesspeople were, the happier they were to meet me and tell me exactly why French leadership was superior to anything the nefarious Brits could imagine. Ask for advice, flatter and the hook has done its job.

Within a firm, most senior managers are delighted to give people the benefit of their wisdom. It costs them little and reinforces their self-image as respected, important and knowledgeable people. Asking for advice gently exploits the vanity of managers, and leads to a more productive conversation than daring to offer advice. The curse of smart people is that they like to show they are smart. Really smart people have the self-confidence to avoid this trap and to appear humble.

If you ask for advice, ask early. Asking for advice is not just about flattering egos. It also works because you give your colleague a sense of control and influence over the outcome. If they control the outcome, they own it. People rarely oppose something which they feel they own and control. The later

> People rarely oppose something which they feel they own and control

you leave the request for advice, the less influence your colleague has over the outcome and the less commitment they will feel towards it.

For instance, I was asked to do a valuation for a bank. I did it and thought I did good work. It was shot down in flames by the bank's financial department. Bank accounts are arcane: the credit crunch suggests that not many bank executives understood their own bank's accounts very well. The high priests of bank finance could shoot down an outsider's analysis of their position with ease. Even if I was right, they could prove that I was wrong. There is a general principle which is never argue with babies, taxi drivers or god: even if you are right it will do you no good. To that list you can add actuaries, financial experts and other technical experts of any kind: never argue with them on their favourite technical subject.

> never argue with babies, taxi drivers or god

Despite that bruising experience, I was asked to repeat the exercise for another bank. This time I made no mistake. Immediately I set up a meeting with the finance department which would review and vet the final valuation. They waxed lyrical about tier 1 and tier 2 capital ratios. I did my best to look interested. I then checked in with them regularly during the assignment to get more advice. By the time we produced the final valuation, they felt it was their valuation. They endorsed it strongly and the board accepted it without question.

Ask for advice early, and keep on asking for it. Share ownership of the final result with anyone who can either derail or endorse the outcome.

The contradiction principle

Sometimes, however, there is an even better way to hook people: encourage them to contradict you. This sounds bizarre, but works in the same way as the advice hook. When they contradict you, they are showing their innate wisdom, expertise and superiority. The trick is to get them to disagree with something you disagree with anyway. They will then vehemently make the case you wanted to present to them. If you had presented the original case to them, the only way they can show their superiority is by picking holes in it. By offering them the chance to contradict you, they make the case on your behalf. They have committed themselves with no effort on your side.

For instance, I decided to do some work on global teams. Most large firms have transnational teams, and most of them struggle. It is a common problem: like my prospective clients I had no idea what the solution was. The challenge was to engage them as clients. If I went to the clients with the problem-solution approach above, I would get nowhere fast. I tried it, and it failed. First, clients would deny they had a problem. Second, they would challenge me for a solution which they would then shoot down. They were not congenial conversations.

So it was time to turn to the contradiction principle. Here is how it was dropped into the conversation at the right moment:

'I am finding lots of my clients struggling to make global teams work . . . mind you . . . your firm has been global so long you must have cracked the problem by now . . .'

This normally leads to a rolling of eyes and a look of sheer disbelief: the client then describes in great detail just what a nightmare it is trying to make global teams work. They make my sales pitch for me. The hook has worked and the way is clear to discussing why global teams are so difficult and what might be done about them. The vehement contradiction leads straight to vehement agreement.

The contradiction principle can be used at any stage of the commitment process. It is a wonderful way of getting people to make your case for you, helping them open up and start talking and letting them reinforce their self-image.

Making commitment a two-way street

Commitment is a two-way street, but is often treated as a one-way street. The goal of the commitment process is to achieve trusted partner status. As trusted partners you will work together as equals towards a common goal. If you are to be equals and you are to work together, you have to establish that mindset from the outset. This is commonly missed. Some people demand commitment and others give commitment without reciprocating. One-way commitments are not healthy and fail to achieve influence.

All of this is obvious, but, as George Orwell once wrote, 'seeing what is in front of your nose requires constant struggle'. The goal is obvious, but many people are unaware of it. And achieving the goal is far harder than stating it. In many cases, commitment lands up as a one-way street.

Most firms have a few sociopaths (which often includes the CEO) who believe commitment is all one-way: they demand complete loyalty and passion and simply do not understand that loyalty has to be reciprocated. For them being a team player means 'you accept my orders or you are not on my team'. 'Give and take' means giving orders and blame, while taking all the credit. These are rarely pleasant relationships, except for the sociopath, who will be very happy with the way the world revolves around himself.

> 'Give and take' means giving orders and blame, while taking all the credit

The more common one-way street is where we are making all the commitment. This is where we play into the hands of the sociopaths and the merely idle. In our desire to impress and show how good we are, we work harder and harder to show what we can do. We land up in a very dysfunctional relationship. Each time we impress, we simply raise expectations. That forces us to work harder than ever, and we get nothing in return. We have not created a partnership of influence; we have turned ourselves into willing slaves. Influence is based on a partnership of mutual commitment and obligation.

To create mutual commitment we have to ask for commitment from the other side: this can feel very unnatural. Most people dislike imposing on others unless there is a clear need. Well, there is a clear need: unless both sides make an effort for each other there can be no partnership of trust. This is as true of marriage partnerships as it is of business partnerships.

The process of mutual commitment has to start from the first meeting: the nature of the relationship needs to be established immediately. The longer you leave it, the harder it is to change the nature of the relationship. In practice, this means you have to ask for something even from the first meeting. It may only be a token effort, but it sets the tone and the expectations going forwards: this is a partnership, not a slave relationship. Here are some simple things I have asked clients to do for me after first meetings:

- Forward a link to an article which the client mentioned
- Clarify a small piece of data which we discussed
- Check, and report, on the views of two colleagues.

These are small tasks which are a big first step. Your partner has made the vital transition from being passive to being active. As a passive counterparty they do little more than act as judge and jury: they may be entertained or even impressed by how well you perform. But they are not helping you perform. They are spectators, not partners, and you will have little influence over them. By making them into active partners, even in a small way, you have set the relationship onto a far more productive path.

As soon as your client or colleague has done some homework for you, they have established a platform for building two-way commitment. You are now in a position to praise and thank them for their work. Giving praise is a power position: it is a positive way of passing judgement. By giving praise you have evened up what may have started as an unequal relationship. You have also created the excuse for reciprocating with a favour of your own and for exploring more ideas. The process of tit for tat has started: the expectation has been set that you will both help each other. The one-way street is becoming a two-way street, but you need to push this new psychological contract further.

> Giving praise is a power position: it is a positive way of passing judgement

At an early stage, set a meeting away from the client's home territory. 'Early' means the second meeting. When the client (or colleague) is in their office they are on their territory. You are the visitor that they have allowed in, and they are the gracious (or not so gracious) host. The guest–visitor relationship is not a partnership. You need to break that mindset fast. Find an excuse to meet on your territory or on neutral territory: in the canteen or at a restaurant. Once they have moved out of their territory, the nature of the relationship changes: you are now more like equals working together. The conversation can change from what you will do for them: it becomes what you can do together. You migrate more easily to the partnership model where you can start to have real influence.

Building a tribe: belonging, meaning and recognition

In many firms loyalty is a one-way street: the firm demands loyalty, passion and commitment right up to the moment where you are right-sized, downsized, offshored, best-shored, re-engineered, outsourced or just plain fired. Unrequited love and unrequited loyalty rarely last long.

loyalty is a one-way street

To sustain commitment, managers need to give as well as take.

There are two basic needs any firm or manager must fulfil to generate voluntary commitment:

● Belonging and meaning: I belong to a community worth belonging to

● Recognition: I am recognised and valued by others for what I do.

Belonging and meaning

The tribal instinct runs deep. We all have a need to belong to a group. The desire to belong is universal. The way we dress proclaims our tribe: the armed forces take great care to show which military tribe everyone belongs to with a range of carefully differentiated uniforms. The corporate tribe has subtle dress codes which vary by type of business, function, level and occasion. Even rebellious teenagers invest a huge amount of time and money acquiring an identity which allows them to belong to one of the ever-shifting tribes of teenage fashion and music. Fortunately, most managers do not have to go to war or become a teenager again to understand and use the power of belonging and meaning.

The power of belonging sustains loyalty in even the most adverse conditions. Sports fans are a good example. For instance, the New Orleans Saints were so unsuccessful in the 1980s they became known as the 'Ain'ts'. Their fans were mortified and some took to wearing paper bags over their heads. They kept on supporting, but it was painful. Sports fans identify with their team: winning teams make their fans feel like winners. Losing teams make their fans feel like wearing paper bags over the heads to maintain their anonymity.

To this day, there are organisations which build extraordinary esprit de corps and gain extraordinary commitment from staff. Many of these are elites: staff at McKinsey or Goldman Sachs feel they are part of an elite and put in huge effort to maintain that status. But you do not have to pay staff vast salaries to create an esprit de corps and a sense of belonging to something special. Soldiers in most British regiments are poorly paid but hugely proud of their regiment and the hundreds of years of tradition they represent. More mundanely, Teach First is an example of how a sense of belonging to something special builds esprit de corps and extraordinary voluntary commitment.

Teach First has perhaps the world's least attractive recruiting proposition for university undergraduates: do not go and get a huge salary at a bank or consulting company. Join us and have two years of grief teaching in the most challenging secondary schools in the UK. Now look at the proposition through another lens. If you join Teach First you will:

- Be joining an elite
- Be trained to be a leader of the future, in education, business or beyond
- Be doing something worthwhile
- Work with other exceptional people like yourself
- Be doing something with high social value and respect: it is supported by prime ministers and royalty alike
- Gain experience which all top employers value greatly: most top recruiters sponsor and support Teach First.

Viewed through this lens, Teach First is highly attractive. Each year 5–10 per cent of Oxford and Cambridge final year undergraduates apply to get onto the programme each year. The messages which Teach First uses are the same that any manager can use to create a sense of belonging:

- We are doing something special and worthwhile
- We are an elite that is capable of achieving this great mission.

In most firms there are teams which clearly look, feel and act as if they are special: they have fierce loyalty to each other and work hard to achieve their goals. It might be a skunkworks developing a new product, or the creative team that develops brilliant advertising, or the IT group which does great things with technology. The two tricks to building this special sense of belonging are:

- Show that the team is doing something special and worthwhile
- Tell the team that they are a special group.

Once people have this sense of belonging their commitment is voluntary and they become self-policing. They perform not because the boss tells them to. They perform because they do not want to let their colleagues down, and they do not want to let themselves down. Peer group pressure is far more intense than boss pressure. Boss pressure is about compliance; peer group pressure is about commitment.

When people have a sense of belonging and meaning, even mundane work becomes meaningful. There is a well-known story of a king going to a building site in the medieval era. He asked the first worker, who looked sullen and unhappy, what he was doing. 'I am getting cold shifting lumps of earth around' came the reply. The king asked a second person the same question. 'Building a building, can't you see?' came the second reply. The king asked a third worker the same question. This worker seemed full of energy and enthusiasm and was working twice as hard as the others. The worker replied with enthusiasm: 'I am serving God and building a temple to Him so that future generations can worship him. This is my monument.' Shifting lumps of earth has little meaning; building a cathedral has great meaning. The same work can be made either meaningless or meaningful. Make work meaningful and commitment rises.

Recognition is a tool which is at the disposal of all influencers. As we look back at the people who have influenced us positively, they are likely to be teachers, parents or even colleagues and bosses who recognised our talents and forgave our very minor defects. We respond well to recognition. Very few people think that they are over-recognised for their talents and contribution: most of us think we are greatly under-recognised and undervalued. That is a wonderful opportunity for an

> most of us think we are greatly under-recognised and under valued

influencer. It allows an influencer to fill a void in someone's life and to stand out from other people who do not give enough recognition.

Recognition is an art form: it can be done poorly or well. Done poorly, it is insincere and sounds insincere. One-minute managers who throw around condescending and generic compliments quickly lose credibility. Good praise is specific, personal and detailed. For instance, if someone helps you:

- explain why the action was useful to you
- explain what was useful about it: what it achieved.

Private recognition is a start: public recognition is even better. To see how influential this can be, we need to observe Francis in action. He is a genius, which means he is smart enough not to show off about how clever he is. If he showed off, he would simply annoy everyone else. Whenever there is a tricky discussion, he stays quiet. He lets all the other brilliant and opinionated people in the room say their piece and argue each other to a standstill. When stalemate has been reached, he will finally speak up and offer to summarise the discussion to date. In the course of his summary he carefully recalls the brilliant insight or contribution of each person around the table: even if they only said one smart thing which he agreed with, he will bring that point back on the table. As Francis makes his summary, you can see each person around the table puff up their chest with pride. They have just been recognised in public for their contribution and insight. By the time Francis has finished his summary, everyone is supporting his summary 100 per cent: no one is going to argue against what they have said. Naturally,

Francis's summary is selective, and it just happens to be a statement of what he wanted at the start of the meeting. But he never has to argue for his position. By giving everyone public recognition he has built their commitment to his idea.

There are plenty of other ways of giving public recognition, even to people who may not be your supporters. Again, we turn to Francis to understand his devious ways of building commitment. Francis wanted to build support for a new market initiative. It was a political nightmare which cut across organisation boundaries and vested interests. After a while I noticed that Francis was producing a trickle of progress updates. In each update he mentioned prominently the magnificent contribution of one or two people who had provided some analysis, insight or support. He was even thanking his opponents. The trick was that he would find one positive amid all the negatives and play that up (while being careful to recognise that they had also identified plenty of other questions to work on). Such public praise helps Francis in three ways:

- It focuses debate on agreements, not disagreements
- It creates an emotional debt to Francis from the people being praised
- It creates the impression of a bandwagon which is starting to roll.

As ever, Francis got his way not through the brilliance of his logic, but through the brilliance of his process. He was building voluntary commitment through recognition and praise. He was converting opponents into allies, which made winning the logical case very simple.

The skill of praising the one positive amidst a sea of negatives is the art of the nice save, which was perfected by P&G. We would be presented with wild, creative, brilliant and utterly useless advertising ideas by our agencies. If we criticised it, the fragile but supersized egos of the creative team would throw a tantrum. So instead we used the nice save. We would identify the one or two positive things about the idea (like they bothered to mention our brand in between the shots of line-dancing hippos in sunglasses). We would get them to work up the good aspects. This would make them more open to sidelining and eventually dropping the hippos. Always look for the positives, give praise and recognition: people become less defensive and more open to change once they feel their extraordinary talents and effort have been properly recognised.

Recognition need not be devious. It can also be simple and direct. John Timpson owns a chain of 400 shoe repair shops which carry his name. Cobbling is not glamorous work. Many of the shops are little more than dark holes in a wall. The key to it is not great cobbling. The key is great customer service. The problem is that cobblers relate to soles more than to souls: they deal with shoes better than they deal with people. Timpson could not regulate great customer service at 400 remote locations. He had to build commitment to it from all the staff. For Timpson, the commitment comes from very public recognition of the right behaviours. He drives around the country with a trunk full of rewards and his goal is to give praise 10 times as much as he criticises: criticism delivers control, praise delivers commitment. He needs commitment because a control and compliance culture does not deliver great customer service. The power of recognition, reinforced with annual awards, newsletters and other public forms of recognition, drive voluntary commitment and the desired service levels.

Gaining commitment by giving control

Management control is seen to be good: managers who are not in control are not doing a good job. From this simple starting point, a whole host of evils emerge. Many managers think that control means reporting, measuring, monitoring, assessing and praising or rebuking. This is control, but it is alienating

staff prefer to be trusted rather than controlled

because staff prefer to be trusted rather than controlled. The growth of technology means that the level of reporting and control today is beyond the wildest dreams of the greatest control freak of years gone by. In the days of pen, paper

Modern management speak talks empowerment but practices control

and the steam train reporting had to be less frequent and less intense. Modern management speak talks empowerment but practises control: we live in an age of distrust.

There is an alternative to heavy management control: self-control and control through peer pressure. These forms of control are voluntary and lead to a commitment culture, not a compliance culture. At a basic level, most people want to stay in control of their lives and their jobs. If we are being controlled by someone else we tend to resent it.

Good influencers use the concept of self-control to induce high commitment and high performance. It is control by letting go, at least to some extent.

The power of control through self-control was very clear in a car factory where I was doing some filming for television. The factory had undergone a TQM revolution: its cars rose from near the bottom of the JD Power reliability ratings to near the top. There are many elements to TQM (total quality management) which experts will wax lyrical about. Elements of TQM can include:

measurement; designing quality in; six-sigma quality; consistency of process; eliminating errors; and not waiting to inspect and fix errors at the end of the process. But on the production line, the revolution was about the people and the nature of control.

Frank had worked at the plant for 30 years. He remembered the bad old days. Supervisors supervised, inspectors inspected and workers were treated as dumb and unreliable machines that had to be monitored closely. It was a compliance culture which encouraged warfare between workers and management: no wonder product quality sucked. With TQM the locus of power shifted. Suddenly, Frank and his colleagues on the line were responsible for quality. At every workstation there was a wall of graphs which showed how they were performing. The data was not the private information of supervisors and inspectors: they had been largely eliminated. This was the public data of each work group. Frank proudly showed me all the data: it was his chance to show how well the team was doing. There was rivalry with other work groups to see who could do best: no one wanted to be the team that was letting the rest of their colleagues down.

With the shift of power and control, Frank and his colleagues saw themselves differently. They were no longer the victims of callous and useless management. They had become champions of quality and production: they were in control of their own destiny. By moving from a compliance to a commitment culture the plant saved itself.

Frank's story is not an exception. In Chicago, an old detergents plant was in trouble. Production for a couple of products was being shifted elsewhere in the group. Another product was being developed by the group, but if the factory wanted it, then they had to bid for it against other factories in the same group. With an old factory and old-style labour relations they looked doomed. Management and workers could not even agree on the length of work breaks, let alone changing working practices enough to win the bid. So management made a radical decision. They decided to leave the factory for six weeks and let the workers figure out if and how they should bid. Six weeks later, the workers had transformed their own working practices and put in a winning bid. They had also redefined the job of management who had to negotiate their way back into the plant. When management controlled the plant, workers had no ownership or commitment. When it was their plant and their problem, they became zealous advocates of best working practices.

The unglamorous world of making pumps in Brazil is not an obvious place to start looking for a management revolution. But Richard Semler, who runs Semco, has become a folk hero for managing by letting go. He claims not to have made a decision in 12 years: the workers make all the decisions: pay, conditions, hiring managers. And it all started with the canteen. As in many firms, everyone liked to whine about the canteen. This annoyed Semler so much that he told the workers they could run the canteen. The complaints stopped and the canteen improved. From that early start, Semler discovered the power of giving control away.

Voluntary commitment is not just about money, as the evidence of the car plant workers, sports fans or any number of voluntary organisations demonstrates. We have to look beyond money if we want to build lasting commitment. This is just as well for most influencers, since we are not normally in a position to bribe colleagues or clients.

Giving control is like delegation. You can delegate away control; you cannot delegate away responsibility. But you change the nature of your role. You no longer add value by ordering, controlling, measuring and assessing. You add value by supporting and coaching, clearing political logjams, securing resources and managing other stakeholders such as top management. In other words, you create

> **You can delegate away control; you cannot delegate away responsibility**

a new role where you add real value to the team, instead of simply being another layer of bureaucracy. Delegating control does not destroy management: it enhances the role of management.

Public commitment, private challenge

Imagine a firm where they have a thorough induction process. First, there is the normal health and safety briefing. Then all the men are taken down to the post room. There, they have to undress. One by one they are led to a blood-stained bench where an evil-looking person gets out a large knife and circumcises them in front of all the other new employees. If anyone cries out in pain, they fail. They are all left there overnight to let their wounds heel. Those who pass have their bodies painted and they then spend the next 30 days going round the office wearing nothing but their body paint. Everyone can plainly see they have passed the circumcision test. After a few more tests, those who pass get to pick a girl from the office. This is a firm which might not recruit many people, but those who joined up would be pretty deeply committed.

This firm is called the Dogon. The Dogon are members of a traditional society that live in the barren scrub of sub-Saharan Mali. The local blacksmith does the circumcising on a blood stained rock. The surrounding rocks are covered in murals: one shows a long snake which will eat anyone who fails the test. Other murals represent different families, and yet more retell the secrets and legends of the Dogon to which the young men will be introduced. The Dogon are not alone in having elaborate rites of passage. Other brutal rites can be found in most traditional societies from Africa to Australia and the South Pacific. Slightly less brutal initiation rites and passing-out ceremonies are common in the armed forces and even fraternities and sororities on campus.

In each society, belonging is not just nice to have: it is essential to survival. To be cast out from such a society means death. Belonging makes it worthwhile for aspiring members of the tribe to go through such unpleasant rites. Equally, the public commitment reinforces the sense of belonging. Public commitment and belonging reinforce each other.

Public commitments are powerful commitments: they offer no going back. For instance, I once made the mistake of deciding to run a marathon. I trained, and then realised it was all too much like hard work and I did not have the time. I dropped the idea. Then I made the same mistake again, with a twist. This time I told four colleagues that I would run. They laughed and told everyone else: when challenged, I confirmed I was going to run. Suddenly, I was committed. There was no going back and no excuses. Letting myself down is not great: letting everyone else down is far worse. So I trained and ran and completed it. And I will never make the same mistake a third time.

The principle of public commitment runs both ways. It can be positive or negative. Once a colleague has taken a position in public, they find it very hard to unwind that position. They will go through more or less any intellectual hoops to justify what they have said or done. The need to self-justify came through clearly with a focus group of owners of outsized off-road vehicles in London. There is not much need for off-road driving in the city. When asked about the environmental aspects of driving such a car in the city, the mood turned ugly. The responses were:

- A car with a family in it is far better than all the buses which never have anyone in them
- Old Land Rovers have the same wheelbase as a new Mini
- We only drive 6000 miles a year, which is far more responsible than people who drive 40,000 miles a year in a smaller car
- At least we don't fly so much
- Electric cars are even worse because of battery disposal and all the power station emissions for powering the batteries

- People are just envious of us
- It's a free society, isn't it?

There is not much logic in any of the answers, but there is a plenty of self-justification. Once people have taken a position, they defend it vigorously. For the influencer, this has two implications:

- Manage conflict in private: do not let anyone take a public stance against your interests
- Publicise agreements and commitments quickly and widely.

Manage conflict in private

Managing conflict in private is a basic requirement of influence. This is especially important where you have a new idea which you want to promote. If you raise your idea in a meeting, say goodbye to your idea. Meetings are designed to kill ideas and to discourage anyone else from daring to have ideas. In the words of one French cabinet minister: 'meetings are a wonderful opportunity to destroy the plans of other ministries.' The last time I made the

> Meetings are designed to kill ideas and to discourage anyone else from daring to have ideas

mistake of having an idea in a meeting, I found myself at the wrong end of a shooting gallery. The bullets all came in the form of helpful questions:

'How much will it cost? Is it in your budget? Whose budget is it? Who will work on it, is anyone available? Have you done a risk assessment? Have you talked this through with HR/Finance/IT/Ops/Japan/my great-aunt's parrot? We've never done this before, so how is it possible? We did it before and it doesn't work, does it? Where's the business case?'

This is the normal reaction to new ideas in meetings. The easiest way to prove you are smart is to ask smart questions and identify the main risks: this has the benefit of protecting the firm against risk. It also kills the idea and removes the need to take any further action. Conversely, encouraging ideas is dangerous and may lead to more work.

Unless you know you have support, keep critical discussions private. The dividing line between a private and public meeting is two people. As soon as there is a third person the meeting is essentially public and each person is taking a position: the discussion becomes a negotiation. In private, people can be more open, more honest and more flexible. If they disagree with you, you can still go back to them another time to address their concerns and find a way forward. Once they have raised doubts in public, they will keep on reinforcing their position. The need for self-justification will overwhelm the need for logic.

There are some basic principles for managing these private disagreements:

- Listen
- Find agreements not disagreements
- Focus on interests, not positions
- Size the prize
- Focus on facts not opinions.

These principles are covered in detail in the following chapters. The common theme behind these principles is that good influencers do not just win an argument: they win an ally. The goal is not to beat your opponent into submission with the brilliance of your analysis. The goal is to find a win–win outcome which both sides like.

Publicise agreements

When you have agreement, make it public. This is where meetings are useful. Meetings should never be used to make a decision: give people a choice and they may make the wrong decision. Meetings should only be used to confirm in public the decisions which have been reached in private. This public confirmation of private deals is vital: it gives reassurance to each individual that they are not alone in giving support to your idea. No one wants to be the first to jump. But with the right choreography, you can persuade everyone to jump at the same time. The meeting is where they jump.

> Meetings should never be used to make a decision: give people a choice and they may make the wrong decision

The 'right choreography' is about building confidence and consensus. The Japanese describe this process as 'nemawashi'. It takes time but is highly effective. Working for a Japanese bank in Tokyo and an American bank in New York showed the power of the process. In Japan, months passed before we finally came to a decision. When we got to the formal decision-making meeting, the decision had already been made. We were simply confirming all the consensus which had been reached in private. Implementing the decision was rapid, smooth and effective.

In New York, we had to meet an urgent deadline and presented our recommendations as soon as we had done the analysis, but without any 'nemawashi'. A riot erupted in the meeting. The decision was pushed through anyway. For months afterwards, the decision was being sabotaged, rival plans were being promoted, power barons were doing their own things. It was a coruscating whirl of activity and initiative. Huge talent and effort was expended in going precisely nowhere. The Japanese tortoise was much faster than the American hare.

The process of building confidence is a search for agreement. The agreement process is incremental. You are managing a series of persuasive conversations (Chapter 12) in parallel. At each stage of the conversation, you are trying to find areas of agreement which allow you to build consensus and confidence.

For instance, one large telecoms company told us that they had a very high-performance culture: it was the secret of their success. We suspected that they had a low-performance culture which was supported by the legacy of a legal monopoly over fixed-line telecoms. The legacy was wearing out and they needed to change the culture. There was little point in arguing about their opinion. So we gathered the following facts:

- Employees were 27 times more likely to die in service than to be fired for poor performance: this was not because all their employees were getting killed, but because no one was getting fired

- 92 per cent of staff were rated as average or above average, which is mathematically impossible

- IBM fires the weakest 10 per cent of its managers every year.

We refused any discussion about the performance culture. All we did for the first few weeks was to validate the findings. We asked the managers to confirm that the facts were correct. When they gave us confirmation, we published the facts and the confirmation. As the deluge of data became overwhelming the claims about being a high-performance organisation simply disappeared. We focused on areas of agreement (facts, not opinions) and publicised the partial agreements: incrementally, we were building commitment and momentum.

Summary

Away from the dramatic speeches by CEOs and gurus about excellence, passion and commitment, the daily life of managers is a hard grind. It can be like swimming through treacle. Dealing with politics, opposition and conflict; making alliances, trying to make a difference while trying to keep day-to-day operations in order.

The commitment process gives a clue as to why management is such hard work. The commitment process takes time and effort. At any one moment a manager can have a dozen commitment conversations on the go with different colleagues: each conversation will happen intermittently over days and weeks. Keeping track of each conversation and orchestrating them so that they all reach the right conclusion at the right time is a fine art and an exhausting sport.

The commitment process may be hard work, but it is a worthwhile investment. Once you have created mutual commitment, you have a platform for success. You will have allies on whom you can rely. In the short term it is possible to persuade and bully people into agreement. Influencers have more ambition than persuaders. Influencers want willing and lasting commitment, whereas persuaders will settle for temporary compliance and acceptance. The commitment process separates out influencers from persuaders.

Part Two

Whispers of influence: acting and looking the part

Chapter 4

Act the part

Try this simple test. Who would you be more likely to trust:

A: Ripped jeans, matted hair, stubble, dirty fingernails, slouching, cynical and mumbling?

B: Well-pressed suit, clean, shaven, attentive, focused, energetic and positive?

If you chose Type B you may have put your trust in bankers who have blown billions while lining their pockets; you may have trusted politicians who buy floating duck houses for their gardens and have their moats cleaned at public expense. And that perhaps makes the point. Type A may be far more trustworthy than Type B, who may all be charlatans, but we are still inclined to trust Type B. Appearances matter. Call it 'career gear' or 'dress for success': first impressions count.

Put simply, if we want to be influential, we have to act and look influential. We need to be perceived the right way. Perceptions may be wrong, but the consequences of those perceptions are real. Perception management is essential.

> Perceptions may be wrong, but the consequences of those perceptions are real

Perception management is a combination of how you behave and how you look. There is argument about how quickly people judge each other when they first meet. Some claim it takes three minutes to form a judgement. Others say it takes just three seconds. Either way, it is clear that first impressions count. With that in mind, we will explore four themes:

- Act the part
- Ambition: the art of unreasonable management
- Look the part
- Make the right first impressions.

Act the part

Every organisation has its unwritten rules of survival and success. You need to decode those unwritten rules for yourself. Some of the common questions include:

- How late should I really work?
- Should I take initiative and risk, or keep my nose clean and follow the process?
- What do I really need permission for, and what do I just get on with?
- How should I dress?
- What sort of jokes can we tell, to whom and when: or are we Very Serious?
- How deferential should I be to the big bosses?

You can search in vain through policy manuals for answers to these questions. Everyone knows the rules, but no one will tell you. They will not even tell you what the questions are: you have to get the answers to the exam right without knowing the questions.

A firm's rules of survival and success are mandatory etiquette. Ignore them at your peril. There is also a huge amount of discretionary etiquette. Much of this relates to cultural differences: don't eat with your left hand or show the soles of your feet in the Middle East; exchange business cards with both hands in Japan. All this discretionary etiquette is useful to know. But foreigners are forgiven even the worst cultural blunders if they display the three Es of influential behaviour:

- Engagement
- Energy
- Enthusiasm.

Engagement: managing with your eyes and voice

Mark was the superstar manager of a chain of electrical goods retailers. I decided to go and see him in action. Watching people work is always more congenial than doing the work.

> watching people work is always more congenial than doing the work

It quickly became obvious that Mark managed with his eyes. He was a one-man masterclass in the art of eye contact. As with most store managers, his eyes were constantly moving to see what was going on: shelf displays needing attention; staff needing help; shoppers wanting to buy. He watched shoppers particularly hard to find the right time to approach them. As soon as they started pointing to or touching a product they were getting warm, but still he waited. As soon as the shopper looked around for help, Mark would be ready to catch their eye; they would be hooked. He would then approach and say 'Hello, I'm Mark the store manager. How can I help you?' The personal introduction made him seem approachable and friendly. The open question (not 'can I help you?' which invites 'no – I'm just looking') also ensured a positive response.

Even as he was talking to his shoppers, he would not lose sight of the rest of the store. He threw instructions with his eyes. If he saw another shopper needing help, he would catch the eye of another shop assistant: the message would be read and the shopper would find a helpful assistant by their side.

Eye contact is very obvious, very powerful and much underused. Billy Graham, the great American preacher, used it to devastating effect. How do you engage hundreds with eye contact? One person at a time, that's how. He did not look blankly at the sea of faces in front of him. Each phrase, each sentence would be addressed directly to one person in the audience. It was electrifying to find that you were being addressed directly and in person by the great man. Once engaged, you stayed engaged.

Use eye contact even when not speaking. Instead of shuffling papers at a meeting, keep your focus on the speaker. You will hear more, understand more and look more engaged than the other people who are scribbling notes, checking mobile phones beneath the table or gazing out of the window. As you look at someone, you will probably find that you unconsciously mirror their body movements. When they lean forward, you will too. This appears empathetic and engaged. Other people who are not engaged may well be leaning back, fiddling about. The more you look at them, the more likely you are to mirror their behaviour and look disengaged. And once you look disengaged, you probably become disengaged as well. The mind switches off when the body does, and vice versa. Choosing where to look has impact.

If you want a change of view, look at the chair. You will probably pick up how they are reacting. And the chairperson will notice you, making it much easier for you to intervene when you want.

Acting the part is not just about using your eyes well. It is also about using your voice well. When you are speaking, speak slowly and with purpose. Research on the great speakers such as Churchill, Kennedy and Mandela shows that they speak much more slowly than most people: nearer 110 words a minute against 120–150 words a minute in normal speech. Martin Luther King spoke just 88 words in the first minute of his 'I have a dream' speech. As an exercise, try repeating his speech at his speed (88 words a minute). And then try saying it at gabbling speed of 250 words a minute. You will still make sense at speed, but the meaning and weight will be lost:

I have a dream

That one day this nation will rise up and live out the true meaning of its creed:

'We hold these truths to be self-evident that all men are created equal'.

I have a dream

That one day on the red hills of Georgia

Sons of former slaves

And sons of former slave owners

Will be able to sit down together at the table of brotherhood.

I have a dream

That one day, even the state of Mississippi,

A state sweltering with the heat of injustice . . .

Going slow adds weight to each word and, by extension, to the speaker. Note also that his speech is full of short words and there is no management jargon. Jargon impresses no one except the speaker. Use plain English: it is more powerful and direct than the contortions of management-speak jargon. By contrast, someone who is speaking at 250 words a minute sounds manic.

> Jargon impresses no one except the speaker

Clearly, if you only ever speak slowly, you will sound odd. It pays to mix it up: varying pace and pitch will keep people engaged. But if you have something important to say, slow right down so that the message comes across with clarity and emphasis.

Energy: the art of positive relaxation

Some people exude energy and other people exude apathy. Energetic people make things happen; apathetic people let things happen to them, and then complain about it. Influential people need to have energy: making things happen requires pushing people and overcoming the natural inertia of the organisation. Without putting energy and effort in, inertia will stop you doing anything.

Sustaining energy and commitment requires belief in what you are doing. If you believe it is worthwhile to yourself, your organisation or the wider community, you can find the reserves of energy to overcome the inevitable setbacks that we all face. If you do not believe in what you are doing, you can keep the momentum going for a while, but it is very hard to sustain for years. Pick the right job, employer, boss and cause.

In the short term, there are a few simple tricks anyone can use to raise their energy levels, without the need for caffeine, sugar and other stimulants. The simplest way to get your energy levels up is to relax your body and adopt the right posture. You can do this even as you wait for a meeting to start or walk towards a meeting. The bigger the meeting, the more important it is to relax: we inevitably get tense before some big event. Tension is very obvious and self-defeating. By looking tense and nervous, we make other people nervous and suspicious about us. If we look relaxed and confident, people pick those signals up and are more inclined to trust and believe us.

You can relax from the head down. Relax the shoulders: the hunchback of Notre Dame look has never been fashionable. Loosen the neck muscles. Stop grinding your teeth (smiles are allowed…). Straighten your spine. Unclench your fists and relax your fingers. Stand with your weight to the front of your foot: imagine that a piece of paper could be passed under your heel. Breathe deeply to get some oxygen into your lungs. If you do all of this, you will find your energy is up, your voice sounds right and you will look calm, confident and relaxed.

Enthusiasm: the art of visualising success

In Britain, enthusiasm is often treated as a certifiable disease. Cynicism is rampant is some organisations. This makes the enthusiast stand out even more. If you are not enthusiastic, do not expect anyone to be enthusiastic for you. If you don't believe in your idea, no one else will.

> enthusiasm is often treated as a certifiable disease

Telling someone to be enthusiastic is as unhelpful as ordering them to laugh and be happy. It is hard to fake. Part of enthusiasm comes from believing in what you are doing. However, you can train yourself to raise your enthusiasm at the right moments.

Think of influencing people as a performance: you are going to make someone agree to something, or see an idea or yourself in a different light by the end of your meeting. They do not know how

you are going to change them: you are in control of this performance. Enjoy it. To visualise it, visualise the end, the start and the
middle in that order.

Visualise what success looks like; what you will be doing and how
you will be feeling at the end of the meeting. This is the success
mindset that is worth carrying into the meeting.

Visualise the start, and then the middle, in as much detail as
possible: what the scene will look, smell, feel like; what you will do
and say to get the meeting off to a successful start; visualise dealing
with all the challenges that may emerge, and the pleasure that will
come from tackling the challenges successfully.

The art of visualisation is about creating a very rich success script
for you to follow. It is not a nice-to-have exercise. It is essential. If
you go into a meeting with no script, then you are either a spontan-
eous genius or you are hoping to get lucky. If you go in with a
script that is full of fear, doubt and anxiety you will find the script
is self-fulfilling. When you play a part, it pays to have the
right script.

Visualisation is a standard technique in high-performance sports.
Watch a goal kicker in the NFL or in rugby and they will take
20 seconds preparing for a one-second kick. The preparation is all
mental and is about visualising what they will do and what success
looks like. They visualise slotting their ball between the posts.
Discretion forbids saying what they imagine lies between the two
posts: it is enough to note that what they imagine motivates them
greatly to score.

Ambition: the art of unreasonable management

Young Alexander inherited a state which was on the edge of Greek
civilisation. It was a tinpot state. Any sane prince would have
recognised this truth and stuck to learning philosophy and

persecuting the local peasants. Ten years later, young Alexander had become Alexander the Great who had conquered all of the known world, and beyond. Great leaders are not modest: does anyone remember his cousin Alexander the Reasonable?

In business, ambition can be a dirty word: to accuse someone of being ambitious is to imply they are naked careerists who are in it for themselves at the expense of everyone else. But business empires are not built by reasonable people: no one in their right mind would have taken on the might of BA, UPS, ABC, IBM or General Motors in their pomp. Without unreasonable leaders like Michael O'Leary, Fred Smith, Rupert Murdoch, Michael Dell or Kiichiro Toyoda, we would never have got Ryanair, FedEx, Fox, Dell or Toyota.

Ambition for your company, your team and then for yourself is good. A simple form of ambition is to ask: 'how does this look to bosses two levels above me?' If it makes no impression on their agenda, you are not making an impact. I learned this lesson when I first presented a promotions plan to the board. I was ready for all the questions about costs, redemption levels, supermarket support, logistics and the rest of the detail I had been sweating over. The board was not interested. They wanted to know things like: will this cannibalise other brands? Will it improve or dilute our brand equity? Can we replicate this internationally? They were big questions to which I had no clue. I had been thinking at the wrong level: they wanted strategy and all I had was detail.

When you are ambitious you set an agenda which resonates across the organisation, not just in your own silo. In this sense, influence is like your credit card. Once you go beyond your formal limit of credit (authority and influence) and you can cope with it, you get invited to extend

> influence is like your credit card

your credit (authority and influence) even further. Bigger and larger opportunities come your way.

Being ambitious means being unreasonable, selectively. You have to push and stretch your team to achieve more than they believe is possible. This is not being mean to them: it is only by stretching them that they develop new skills and new capabilities. There are, clearly, limits to the art of unreasonable management. Unreasonable management should not be about hectoring, finger wagging, and demeaning people. To be unreasonable and ambitious effectively, managers should:

● Be firm about the goals, flexible about the means

● Support and enable the team at all points

● Give the team a sense of control: the difference between pressure and stress is control. If I have pressure and no control over my fate, I feel stress. If I feel pressure but remain in control I will stretch and develop

the difference between pressure and stress is control

● Read the warning signals: if the team shifts from pressure to stress, lead them straight back down the mountain to their comfort zone. Let them reacclimatise before leading them back again.

To be influential, managers must make a difference, and that requires ambition.

Look the part

There is an old adage which says that you are never poorly dressed if you wear a smile. The implication is that personality shines through: we do not judge purely by appearances. I had an opportunity to test this theory in my final year at university. Procter & Gamble summoned me to an interview on campus. Unfortunately, my appointment clashed with the need to build a theatre set. So I compromised. I rushed from the theatre, in my oily, paint-speckled overalls, straight into the interview. Because I was busy, I did not have time to get nervous, let alone get changed. I may have looked a mess, but I played a part to perfection. In a miserable theatrical career, it was the only part I played with success. It worked because I was true to myself at that moment: I was energetic, enthusiastic, committed and clearly doing something interesting. After recovering from shock, my interviewer hired me. Whether that was a wise choice is still in dispute.

If we have the right behaviour, we can survive most sartorial blunders. But we should not make it hard for ourselves. If we dress the part, it makes it far easier for people to believe us.

In some cases, it is very easy to follow the dress code and look authoritative. The armed forces give their senior officers plenty of gold braid and medals. Their crisp uniforms exude crisp authority. I discovered the full power of dress when I ventured into the highlands of Papua New Guinea. I first met the tribe in a ramshackle town. The tribesmen were wearing their best clothes for town: second-hand clothes inherited from Western charity donors. They looked evil. I had no idea who their leader was: they all looked as menacing as each other.

Two days later I reached their village in the distant highlands. They changed out of their town clothes. Suddenly, it was easy to see who the chief was. He was the one with a headdress made of huge bird-of-paradise feathers, and he was bedecked in cowrie shells and other exotic imports from the coast. He looked magnificent, even regal. In town he had looked like a tramp or potential mugger. Same person in different dress gave a different message.

In the business world it is perhaps best not to wear gold braid, medals and bird-of-paradise feathers in your hair. We need some other way of appearing authoritative and influential. The problem is that dress codes are becoming ever more ambiguous. There has been a sartorial revolution since the days when grey socks would have been seen as subversive. At a recent conference of a global high-tech firm, everyone from the CEO downwards wore jeans and T-shirts. The dress code was as clear at P&G, but radically different. Conformity simply had a different code.

The principles of dress codes are the same as the principles of all etiquette. Etiquette is not about arcane rules over where to put the fish knives. Etiquette should be about providing rules which put everyone on an equal footing, and put everyone at ease. The same goes for dress codes. The goal is to put your colleagues at ease: they should feel comfortable being seen with you and talking to you. Given the variety and ambiguity of dress codes, there is no simple answer to how you should appear. However, there are some guiding principles:

● Mirroring: conformity

● Conservatism

● Aspiration.

Mirroring and conformity is the key principle: dress how others dress. If everyone else is dressing in T-shirt and jeans, you should probably follow. Dressing in a suit and tie would mark you out as a stuffy weirdo. Equally, if you go to a formal black-tie event, wearing a T-shirt and jeans is simply insulting to everyone else who has made the effort to dress up. T-shirts and formal suits are simply different styles of conformity.

> T-shirts and formal suits are simply different styles of conformity

Conservatism: if in doubt, err on the side of caution and formality. This applies particularly to people who are down the pecking order of power: suppliers, vendors and junior staff. For instance, consultants tend to dress slightly more conservatively than their clients. They need to look trustworthy and reliable. All the greatest rogues, from bankers to tyrants and politicians, dress in sober suits and ties. It is their camouflage to make them appear trustworthy. It works all too often.

Aspiration: this is particularly useful for more junior staff. Look at how people one or two levels above you dress. The chances are they spend more money, time and effort on their personal appearance. If you want to join the club, it pays to follow the club dress rules. If in doubt, mirror the example of senior people, not junior people. Judging people on how they dress is both absurd and unfair, but who said the world was fair?

First impressions

If you know how to look and act the part, you are well on the way to making a good first impression. But special situations require special preparation. Two occasions when you will need to make a strong first impression are:

- Meeting someone for the first time (selling or interviewing, for instance)
- Making a presentation.

Meeting someone for the first time

I found myself responsible for recruiting business school graduates to a high-end strategy firm. Some candidates were easy: they were great or they were disasters. Most were in the middle: they seemed to tick all the boxes, but we could not make our minds up about them. I found a very easy way of making the decision: I asked my secretary, who would have walked them to and from reception. It only took a couple of minutes, but most candidates revealed themselves in that time, with their defences down. Assuming that secretaries do not matter is a fatal error. Subsequent events indicated that she had about a 90 per cent success rate in picking winners, which was better than the rest of the selection team put together.

Here is what she looked for:

- *The three E's*: energy, excitement and enthusiasm. Even if they were nervous, that was OK, as long as they had the three E's.

- *The fourth E:* expertise. Did they actually know anything about our firm? Some candidates showed total ignorance. Others used the walk to slip in a couple of insightful questions, hoping to get a reality check from the secretary. Smart move, much appreciated.

- *The fifth E*: engagement. Some candidates took the time to exchange pleasantries with my secretary and treat her like a human being. Others behaved as if she was invisible and did not matter. She was visible and she did matter, as they later found out to their cost.

If you have the five E's it is quite hard to go far wrong. If in doubt, let people talk about their favourite subject: themselves.

Making a presentation

The three E's of energy, excitement and enthusiasm go far in any presentation. Long after people have forgotten what you said, they will remember how you were. If you dress like a tramp and are king of the mumblers, do not expect a great reception. To achieve the three E's of energy, excitement and enthusiasm, there are two more E's worth having: expertise and enjoyment. Know what you are talking about. And if you enjoy what you do, that will come across clearly to the audience.

In truth, most corporate presentations are dire. Bigwigs use presentations to fill the air with nothing more than their own self-importance. More junior staff inflict death by detail and the pain of PowerPoint on their audiences. They have highly sophisticated and complicated slides which they read more slowly than the audience can read the same slides.

This is terrible news for people who have to sit through such presentations. It is wonderful news for managers who want to make a difference, influence and be seen positively. With such dire competition it is easy to stand out. A few basic disciplines help you succeed where others fail:

- Smart presenter, dumb slides: Slides should do no more than mark where you are in the conversation. The presenter can then show brilliance and insight by adding commentary to each slide.

- Short is good: a presentation is not complete when no more can be said. It is complete when no less can be said. Presentations, like diamonds, benefit from good cutting.

- Tell a story. Your presentation should be a journey: this is where we are, this is where we are going, this is how we will get there. Take your audience on a journey. Make it interesting.

- Take the part of the listener: Focus on what they need and want to hear, not what you want to say. This will help you cut the presentation down to size.

- Focus on a few key people: in a room of 100 people, there may be three or fewer people you need to influence. Focus everything on those few people.

- Make it memorable. Find a few killer facts, a stunning story or a few memorable phrases which give your listeners hooks by which to remember you and your message. These hooks will also help you structure the flow of your talk: they will act as staging posts in your flow.

- Stand up properly: keep the weight slightly on the front of your feet. Don't let your posture sag. You will look as though you have lost energy and interest. If possible, stand and relax before starting, so that you are ready to go.

- Script your first 20 seconds, so that you can make a confident start. Memorise your last 20 seconds so that you can make a great finish. Throw away the rest of the script: it will make you look and sound wooden.

- Visualise the whole event beforehand in as much detail as you can.

- Prepare, and then prepare some more. Then prepare again. Finally, keep preparing. Arrive early so that all the logistics are right for you.

Summary

All organisations are tribal, and all tribes have their own rituals which they jealously guard. No one set of dress or behaviour is better than another. All that matters is whether you choose to conform to the tribal rituals or rebel against them. Even rebellion is many organisations is ritual: shocking socks with a sober suit is a highly conformist rebellion.

But there is a limit to conformity. Many firms become a sea of greyness. The way to stand out as an island of Technicolor amid such greyness is to show energy, enthusiasm and excitement for what you do. You can only do this if you enjoy what you do: we only excel at what we enjoy. If you dare to show all these E's (excitement, energy, enthusiasm, expertise and enjoyment) you will stand out much more than the individuals with the loud socks, and you will stand out for the right reasons.

> we only excel at what we enjoy

Chapter 5

Active listening

liked to think I was a great salesman. I had sold my own blood in Afghanistan. I was the best nappy salesman in Birmingham. I had even sold a bank. I had the patter; I could browbeat any buyer into submission; I knew all the tricks, could counter all the objections and would always close the sale.

And there was one salesperson I hated. She was useless. She had no charisma, no patter, no tricks, nothing. But she always outsold me and could sell anything to anyone. It was infuriating.

Eventually, I got to see her in action. I was gobsmacked. She had no patter. She hardly talked. She just sat there and listened to the buyer. She admired all the trivial triumphs he boasted about. She empathised with all the minor disasters and crises he had faced. She just let him talk about himself. It was a complete waste of time. She was not selling our services. Our scheduled hour was running out and I had to run to another meeting. An hour and half later I returned. They were still talking and she was still listening: the buyer had postponed his other meetings so he could carry on. He clearly liked talking about his favourite subject: himself.

> he clearly liked talking about his favourite subject: himself

At last, the buyer exhausted himself and said, 'I suppose we ought to talk about that bid....' Even as he said it, it was clear he had made his mind up. He was going to give it to her. He trusted her because she clearly understood him and respected him, unlike all the other salesmen who had come in trying to browbeat him into submission: she was the only person that appeared to be on his side. It was not even a contest: she was the only runner left in the race.

I may have fancied myself as a world-class seller: she was a world-class listener. I discovered that listeners can beat sellers every time in the influence game. Sellers, at their worst, engage in competitive and adversarial relationships: the seller wins and the buyer loses, and on bad days the roles are reversed. Buyers recognise this relationship and act accordingly: they are defensive, aggressive and not at all cooperative.

> Good leaders have two ears and one mouth, and use them in that proportion

Listeners bypass all the buyer's defences. They encourage collaboration and partnership. Buyers want to work with people who listen. I had learned a basic lesson. Good leaders, salespeople and influencers have two ears and one mouth, and use them in that proportion. They listen twice as much as they talk.

Salespeople tend to be hunters; listeners tend to be farmers. History tells us that farmers win over hunters: not many hunting societies are left today. The hunting mindset is a series of discrete events: each sale is a transaction, a chase to victory or defeat. Success or failure yesterday has little bearing on success or failure tomorrow. The farming and listening mindset is different. It is about cultivating win/win relationships. Once the relationship of trust is established, it plants the seeds of success which can be harvested tomorrow. Farming is an investment in the future which pays handsome dividends tomorrow. Hunters live for today.

Good listening is effective for several reasons:

● You find out about the person who is talking: what matters to them, what they like and dislike, what they need.
They are giving you the information you need to influence them effectively

- People like talking about themselves, their job, their challenges
- Listening builds trust and rapport: you appear to be on their side, as opposed to talkers who seem to follow their own agenda.

Good listening may be effective, but it is also an art form. You cannot just sit down and hope that a stranger will start discussing their personal lives with you. Strangers who do this are often well worth avoiding, especially on public transport.

There are five principles to effective listening which we will explore in detail:

- Open and purposeful questions
- Reinforcement: the coffee shop principle
- Paraphrasing
- Contradiction
- Disclosure.

Open and purposeful questions

When we first meet someone, it is very tempting to tell them who we are. It is human nature to puff ourselves up a little: we want to make a good impression and show that we are someone who is worth talking to. The problem with this approach is that it is B-O-R-ing. We may be a source of endless fascination to ourselves, but strangers really do not care. So turn this logic around. Ask the person you are meeting to talk about the most interesting subject on the planet: themselves. The simplest way to do this is to ask the Queen's question (she asks this question on walkabouts when meeting the great unwashed): 'what do you do?' There are more creative ways of asking the same question. Having studied tribes for years, I sometimes ask people what tribe they come from. Most people see their firm as a collection of tribes and dive straight into telling me all about their tribes and how they have to fight the other tribes and departments.

Once they have started talking, keep them talking. Do this by asking open but directed questions.

An open question is one where it is impossible to reply yes/no: it encourages a rich answer. Open questions will often start 'How, what, why…' For instance:

● How does this work?

● What are the major risks/benefits of this?

● Why are they trying to stop this?

Each of these questions will encourage a rich reply. In contrast, closed questions invite a yes/no answer and may well kill off the discussion. The three open questions above can be posed as closed questions:

● Will this work?

● Is this worthwhile?

● Will they stop this?

These closed questions are very dangerous. The answer may not only be short: it may be the wrong answer. So if you ask 'will this work?' and the answer is 'no' you have a problem. Suddenly, the onus is on you to prove that it will work. But your colleague has already taken a position that it will not work. So now you are in an adversarial position and your colleague is not talking. You are not back at square one: you are in completely the wrong place if you want a productive conversation. If you ask 'how will this work?' you get a much more useful reply. Perhaps the answer is 'it will only work with great difficulty and under these conditions…' but at least you have a constructive dialogue about how to make it work, rather than an argument about whether it will work.

Clearly, open questions are not random questions. There has to be purpose and direction behind your discussion. The art of the persuasive conversation is covered in detail in Chapter 12. It is enough to make the point and illustrate it here. Take the question above:

- What are the major risks/benefits of this?

You have a choice: ask about the risks first or the benefits first. Your choice of order is likely to determine the success or otherwise of the conversation. If you ask for the risks first, you will get a very rich answer. People are normally risk-averse and are very good at spotting risks. You will get a long list of real and imaginary risks. By the time you have heard the answer, there will be little point in asking about the benefits of the idea. The idea will have been crushed under the weight of all the risks and problems which came to light.

If you ask about the benefits first, you may find that you have to push and probe to get all the benefits of the new idea fully articulated. But establishing why the idea is a good idea changes the nature of the discussion. If the idea is rich in benefits, then it becomes worthwhile dealing with all the risks that you later identify. Your colleague will have invested personal time and effort in establishing that the idea is good, and will be less inclined to drop the idea. By identifying the benefits of the idea, your colleague will have taken ownership of the idea. People rarely oppose their own ideas.

> People rarely oppose their own ideas

Reinforcement: the coffee-shop principle

Go down to your local coffee shop and watch people gossip. You may be able to persuade your boss that this is not just a break from work: it will help your work.

First, watch the body language. You will see that people who are deeply engrossed in conversation mirror each other's body shape. When one leans forward, the other leans forward. If one crosses his legs, the other will as well. It is like ballet without a choreographer. Everyone does it quite naturally.

Now pretend to read a newspaper while you eavesdrop on the conversations. The gossips will be busily supporting and reinforcing each others' world views. Right on cue, they will show delight, disgust, shock, surprise or sympathy with every latest revelation. They will not disbelieve what they are being told, at least not until they recount the story to someone else later. They are making it very easy to talk to each other. They are allies with common interests and common perceptions.

The same principles of reinforcement apply to business conversations. If you want someone to talk, make it easy for them to talk. Show that you are in tune with them and that you are on their side.

Start with the body language. Listening to other people's triumphs and disasters may be boring, but stay focused. Look interested. Make eye contact and stay alert: people quickly pick up lack of interest. Focus 100 per cent of your attention on the person who is talking: when your mind wanders off to planning the next meeting, worrying about your expenses claim and other matters, it shows. When you are focused, people feel flattered and will open up.

Now focus on what you say. You do not need to say much. Copy the coffee shop gossips: show that you empathise and agree with the other person. The moment you challenge them, they will close down and stop seeing you as a friend and ally. Reinforcement helps you build the rapport you need when you move on to more substantive discussions.

Paraphrasing

Paraphrasing is a useful way of showing understanding and building agreement. It can also be used to stop people repeating themselves.

Paraphrasing is simply a summary of what someone has said to you, expressed in your own words. This simple act achieves several goals at the same time:

- It shows that you have listened properly, and that builds empathy with the talker who wants to be heard
- If you have misunderstood, you will quickly be corrected
- It forces the listener to listen actively: you will look interested and the talker will respond positively to your apparent interest
- It helps you remember key information after the meeting: the act of saying something commits it to your short-term memory without the intrusion and formality of a notebook and pen. Opening a notebook closes a conversation: people are rarely open when they are on record.

> Opening a notebook closes a conversation

Paraphrasing needs to be done with some care. If you say 'so what I hear you say is… ' and you then repeat their words exactly you will sound like an insincere automaton. Be authentic. Use your own words to summarise what has been said. That shows you have really listened and internalised what has been said: you are more than a parrot.

For influencers, paraphrasing is most useful in one-to-one meetings where you want to build rapport. It can also be used in group meetings. We have already heard Francis's story. He summarises what everyone says in a meeting selectively: everyone likes what Francis says because it reflects what they have said (at least in part) and so everyone agrees with his selective summary of the meeting. He gets his way without ever having to argue for it.

Finally, paraphrasing makes windbags shut up. We have all been in meetings where there is one person who keeps on making the same point, in different

> paraphrasing makes windbags shut up

ways, time and again. Everyone tries to shut him up. The more people try to stop him talking, the more he feels the need to make his point again because he feels he has not been heard. Instead of attacking such people, work with them. Let them have their say (concisely) and then summarise what was said. Even write it up on a flip chart. You have now amply shown that their point had been made and they have been heard. They can now let the meeting move on.

Contradiction

It was election time. We had 24 hours before the polls opened and we needed to get a last-minute leaflet designed, printed and distributed overnight. And we had more or less run out of budget. No printer was going to take on a low-cost job, overnight and at great inconvenience. I called a printer and got the predictable reply: 'no.' We were stuck. Then I remembered the contradiction principle.

I went round to a printer who had worked for us before and did the normal business of establishing rapport, asking a few open questions. And then he asked, 'What can I do for you?'

'I doubt you can do anything, frankly. I have tried a couple of printers round here and they say it is impossible.'

'What's impossible?' the printer asked. He sounded slightly offended that anyone could doubt his professional expertise and his ability to do anything.

'Well,' I said reluctantly. 'It's this leaflet. Still needs final design. Eight thousand copies by tomorrow morning. I am told no one can do that in that amount of time.'

'Rubbish!' replied the printer, who was now indignant that anyone could doubt his capability. By this time he was fully committed to proving me wrong, at any cost. Even when he heard of the pitiful budget, he was going to show me what he was capable of doing.

Mission accomplished: leaflet printed on time and to budget. Election won.

Contradiction is not about arguing with people. It is about letting people show off. Let them show how good they are. Let them prove you wrong. Contradiction is a powerful principle to use with professionals who are normally more than keen to showcase their professional talent. The trick is to make the contradiction non-confrontational: depersonalise it. Avoid saying 'I don't think this is possible' or 'I don't believe this is true.' That simply invites a win/lose argument. Since they are they experts, they will win.

In similar fashion we have seen how I used the contradiction principle to sell consulting work. Trying to prove that the client has a problem with global teams is impossible for an outsider. Instead I show that other global companies have this problem. This makes it safe for them to admit to having the same problem. Then I say something like: 'Of course, I assume you have cracked this problem: I would be delighted to hear how you have done it... ' This then provokes a reaction of sheer disbelief. They tell me how problematic their global teams are. Job done, and they have done the selling for me.

The goal is contradiction, not conflict. The key to achieving this delicate balance is to depersonalise the contradiction by saying things like: 'Other printers say it is impossible to do this' or 'Finance department say this profit forecast is wrong....' By doing this, you displace the blame and opprobrium onto other people: you can now work together to prove the rest of the world is wrong. You become allies, not adversaries.

Disclosure

A very tedious dinner engagement loomed. A colleague decided to spice it up with a wager. She bet that she could make everyone round the table, before the evening was over, to reveal how they lost their virginity. Easy money. I wagered a modest amount and looked forward to collecting at the end of the evening, No one is going to reveal such intimate details to relative strangers. No chance, no way, never.

By the end of the evening, I was poorer financially and richer in knowledge. I had also disclosed a little more about myself than was perhaps wise.

Maria started by doing what she did best: asking open questions about people, reinforcing other guests by showing interest and empathy. As the evening wore on and the wine flowed, she steered the conversation to slightly more risqué areas. Occasionally, to encourage disclosure she would drop a personal indiscretion into the conversation. Competitively, the other guests would drop in even greater indiscretions. The evening was rapidly becoming more and more entertaining. Both the wine and the disclosures flowed faster and faster.

Perhaps inevitably, the discussion turned to sex. Maria told a funny story against herself. Others followed. Eventually and quite naturally, she found herself saying how she had lost her virginity. Like clockwork, everyone else followed, with suitably extravagant embellishments. Under these circumstances, I could not be the prude who said nothing. I duly followed. Social pressure made disclosure inevitable.

The moral of this tale is not that you influence strangers by telling them how you lost your virginity. The moral is that disclosure encourages disclosure.

Disclosure is a subtle art. It can be done badly. At social events it is common to spot alpha males fighting like rutting stags. They do it through competitive disclosure. They want to outdo each other's anecdotes: who went on the most exotic holiday, who went to the most prestigious conference, who knows the most important people and who has the most air miles. Disclosure needs to be slightly more subtle and self-effacing. Tell enough to make the other person want to disclose. Let them 'win' by giving you a bigger, better and more extravagant story than yours. Never threaten or challenge their stories, even if they appear to be 98 per cent fiction.

Summary

Listening is not a passive art. It requires skill, focus and effort to make other people talk constructively, build rapport and to become a trusted partner. No one becomes a good listener overnight. It takes effort and practice. Remember the five principles of good listening:

- Open and purposeful questions
- Reinforcement: the coffee shop principle
- Paraphrasing
- Contradiction
- Disclosure.

Experiment with each of the principles, one at a time. In time, they will become natural reactions.

Perhaps the easiest starting point is to avoid the three most common mistakes:

- Talking over other people
- Asking closed questions
- Indulging in competitive anecdotes.

These are natural, but unhelpful. If you avoid these traps, you have already made a start. Talking over people and competing with anecdotes springs from the natural desire to impress. They do not impress: they irritate. Short of sticking tape across your mouth, it can be hard not to talk or compete. Even if it causes you to get blood blisters on your tongue, avoid the temptation. Instead, ask open questions and let your colleagues talk themselves into agreeing with you and admiring you.

Chapter 6

Give to take

Generosity is a scarce commodity. As business grows harder and meaner, generosity becomes ever scarcer. As generosity becomes scarcer, it becomes more valuable. This is good news for influencers. A little generosity goes a long way: it is easy to stand out from the crowd of more self-interested colleagues. Influencers take a longer-term perspective: generosity is all about self-interest in the long term. It helps build willing partners, supporters and allies.

A little generosity goes a long way

generosity is all about self-interest

There are two sorts of generosity. The most common sort of generosity builds popularity. There is another sort of generosity which builds influence and power. We need to know which is which.

To understand generosity as popularity we need to look at Sue's story. Sue was, by some distance, the most popular PA on the executive floor. Everyone would stop to talk to her, from the mail man to the CEO. She always had a ready smile and easy banter. She also always had a large bowl of sweets by her desk and had a habit of bringing in cakes to celebrate birthdays, weddings, holidays, Fridays: any excuse would do. Looking at her, it appeared that she was often the main beneficiary of her largesse, but that was all part of her character and appeal. After about a year, her boss got moved to another division: both Sue and the boss agreed that it was not the right thing for her to make the move as well. In the subsequent reorganisation, disaster struck. No one wanted to have Sue as their PA. She may have been popular, but she was not a very good PA. She left to spread her goodwill and smiles elsewhere. It was a sad parting for everyone involved, which they tried to celebrate with a final cake in the office.

Sue was, without question, generous and popular. But she was clearly not influential or powerful. Cakes, sweets and gossip are not the route to influence for any manager. For managers, generosity has to take another form.

Influential generosity is marked out by four characteristics. It should be:

- Customised, not generic
- Earned, not unearned
- Measured, not unlimited
- Requested, not unrequested.

As we shall see, these principles count because they maximise the chances of the generosity being valued and reciprocated. If generosity is neither valued nor reciprocated then we may find ourselves wearing Sue's shoes: we become popular but dispensable. If we follow the right principles, we can acquire allies and supporters who will help us when we need help.

One example will show how to be generous effectively. A senior manager wanted me to move into her department. I did not know her well, although she appeared to be doing interesting work. I had other commitments and was not very interested in listening to her overtures. Eventually, she persuaded me to do a small presentation to her team on my current work. It was a chance to show off; it was easy to do and I was allowed to pick the time and place for the presentation. Easy give. And I was being set up without knowing it.

At the presentation everyone was very kind and flattering. They at least pretended to look interested and impressed. A few days later, a bottle of fancy champagne arrived on my desk: the senior manager had done her homework and had even found out which brand I liked most. I rarely bought it because it was so expensive. It was a gift which scored a bullseye on three of the four principles of generosity:

- It was highly customised to my interests and needs: it showed that she cared. My existing boss had no clue what I liked or did not like, and did not seem to care.

- The gift felt like it had been earned, and so I valued it. It was not just a gift: it was recognition of work well done, and recognition is always welcome. Recognition seemed to be a foreign land to my current boss.

- It was a measured gift: she did not shower me with presents. That would have been crude bribery. This was much more subtle bribery. It set the expectation that I could not get something for nothing: rewards had to be earned.

She then asked me for another favour, helping her on an existing project. I helped and was given more recognition. She had set up the process of give and take. Incrementally, I was being committed to her and split from my existing boss. After a couple of months I willingly made the switch.

Give to take is a powerful way of building commitment. Let's see how the four principles of give to take can be applied in practice.

Custom, not generic, generosity

Generosity pays. For example, we were at a partners' meeting. There were over 1000 of us in a huge conference hall. It felt like a plenary session of the old Soviet Communist Party: all the comrades were expected to raise their hands and approve the decisions of other comrades, proving that neither partners nor comrades are ever truly equal. Managing the show was a huge effort. Deep in the bowels of the building there was a troupe of harried secretaries sorting out all the last-minute crises. Inevitably, they had an endless stream of pompous partners passing their way demanding immediate resolution of vexatious logistics, communications and other problems. I could see their hearts sink when I approached: they saw another problem looming. I went in and thanked them for all their thankless work. They waited for the real reason for my visit, the impossible request I was going to make. There was no ulterior motive. I just thanked them. I left them dumbstruck. Back in the office, I suddenly found all the secretaries being unusually helpful: hard-to-meet executives suddenly had free space in their diaries, life became easy. I later learned that I was the only one of over 1000 partners who had bothered to recognise them and thank them for their efforts.

At the end of the same meeting the CEO (senior partner) summoned the organising secretaries on stage, thanked them and gave them all bouquets of flowers. It was a case study in how not to be generous. Far from being grateful, the secretaries were embarrassed and annoyed. The CEO's gesture failed because:

- It was generic generosity. There was no thought about what the staff might want. They got flowers at the end of every conference, even although they could not fly home with them. There were many gifts the staff might have wanted: the CEO did not know what they wanted, and did not even know most of their names. Generic generosity appears synthetic and insincere.

- The staff had been told to buy their own flowers and put them on expenses. They then handed the flowers to the CEO offstage. He walked on stage and handed the flowers right back to them. There was no hint of personal generosity or effort about the gift. Again, it failed to pass the test of being personal and customised.

- It was ritual. It was what happened at the end of every conference. It failed the test of being unexpected. Further, the ritual simply served to embarrass the staff who preferred not to be paraded on stage like some curious exhibit.

Effective generosity is customised both to the giver and the taker. A mentoring relationship is the classic form of customised generosity because:

- The mentor is giving up personal time and effort
- The mentor is focused completely on the specific needs of the person asking for advice.

For example, when I first stumbled into the world of consulting I had no idea what I was doing. The wags will argue that nothing has changed. There were three founding partners. All were formidable intellects. One of them liked to eat analysts and junior consultants for breakfast. He was brilliant, but terrifying. He also found it very hard to get any staff for his projects: no one could meet his standards, and no one wanted to work for him. No one wanted to be his breakfast. He landed up working himself into an early grave. The other two were just as sharp, but they always seemed to have time for people. They did not boss; they did not humiliate. They listened, supported and helped. They were generous with the one thing that busy people really do not have enough of: their own time. As a result, everyone wanted to work with them and for them. They were time-generous not only with staff, but with clients. They were always prepared to listen, help and support a struggling client. It was all part of the service, regardless of whether there was a paid assignment or not.

Staff and clients flocked to these two partners. They came to rely on their generous, wise and committed support. Not surprisingly, this turned out to be a success formula. Clients have remained with them for 20 years or more; staff remain loyal over decades. Staff and clients who abused their generosity fell by the wayside.

Freeloaders found it harder to open the partners' diaries. But there are many more who have been very happy to reciprocate. Clients always turn to these two partners when there is paid work to be done, and staff are always willing to work on projects led by the two partners.

Generosity is not just about chocolates and champagne. These things have monetary value, but not necessarily personal value. The most precious resources in an organisation tend to be things like time and recognition. When you give people your time, you are investing your most precious and limited resource in them: people respond to that vote of confidence. When you give them recognition, that is also a vote of confidence in them. Once you have made the investment, you can expect to ask for a return on that investment: most people will give willingly. You have set up the process of give to take.

Earned, not unearned, generosity

If you go into a senior banker's office, it is not uncommon to see it full of tombstones. These are not the product of some weird fetish involving graveyards: even bankers have not fallen that far, yet. The tombstones are little Perspex mementoes that are shaped like tombstones. They enclose a piece of paper which records various financing deals they have put in place and have been announced in the financial press. The value of each tombstone can be measured in pennies, and yet rich bankers display them proudly as valuable trophies. The trophies are valued because they represent hard-won triumphs and are a record of their achievement. They have pride of place in the office. If you gave the same banker a nicely designed Perspex paperweight with your company logo on it, the banker would probably put it straight into the number 1 file: the waste basket.

we value what we earn more than what is free

As a general rule, we value what we earn more than what is free. In running a sales force I found salesmen would compete viciously to win the monthly prize, which would often be pretty much a token: perhaps a nice pen or a dinner out. At the annual conference the salesmen would be inundated with free pens and meals: they were worthless. The conference pen lacks meaning or value. The monthly prize may have modest financial value, but has huge symbolic value. It shows who is top dog for the month. It is very public recognition for achievement.

Measured, not unlimited, generosity

The more you give, the less it will be valued. For this, think of Mars Bars. If you give one to a child to eat, the child will be happy. The second will also be quickly accepted. The greedier children may be able to get through the third Mars Bar. By the time child is confronted with

> The more you give, the less it will be valued

the fourth, fifth or sixth Mars Bar, they will be groaning. The seventh Mars Bar will be as welcome as the plague. Be measured in your generosity. What is scarce is more valued than what is abundant. Diamonds and coal are both carbon: scarcity dictates which is more prized.

If we give and continue to give unconditionally, we can quickly become exploited. I helped one charity and they started asking for more and more help which I was happy to give. Eventually, they were consuming half my time and I was being asked to do things which they could have done by hiring someone on minimum wages. I had simply become free labour to be used whenever they could not be bothered to do something themselves. I told them I would do 2–3 days a month in future: suddenly, they worked out how to use me to get most value out of me.

Clearly, there is a balance to be struck. If you give too much, you will be taken for granted and exploited. If you only give in return for something, then that is not generosity: that is trading. The key is timing. Be generous early. First impressions count. Early acts of generosity mark your character. Do not ask, or even expect, anything in return for a while. If you ask for something back, you have become a trader and you have ceased to be generous.

Over time it will become clear who are freeloaders that want to exploit you, and who are prepared to reciprocate. You do not need to argue or complain to the freeloaders. As your flow of generosity dries up, they will quietly disappear. You can focus on those people with whom you can build a more productive relationship.

Measured generosity requires clarity about who to help, how to help and how much to help. That means learning to say 'no' to requests for help. This can feel awkward. But it is far better to say no than commit to doing something and doing it poorly. Poor work destroys personal credibility, even if it was done generously out of your discretionary time and effort. Only agree to help if you have the relevant capability (skill), capacity (time) and will (you want to help). 'No' may be hard to say, but saves tears later. There are three principles to saying no gracefully:

- Be clear about your decision: lack of clarity leads to disaster and mismatched expectations later. If you appear unreliable you lose credibility, trustworthiness and influence.

- Be clear and honest about why you cannot do it: most people will respect your decision if they understand why you are making it. If you lack the capability or capacity to help, say so.

- If possible, offer an alternative. Perhaps you can help later, or someone else may be more expert, or you may be able to help with just part of the problem. Offering an alternative at least shows some goodwill.

Requested, not unrequested, help

There is a phrase which sends a chill down the spine of any practising manager: 'Hello. We're from head office and we are here to help you.' This is the sort of help which has your finances, operations and staff being turned upside down and inside out. Imposed help is rarely helpful. It is interference, not help.

Despite this, unrequested help flourishes. Managers help their teams with unwanted reviews, coaching, advice and direction. Colleagues help each other with advice. This can be lethal. In the executive suite there is an informal no pissing rule: 'I will not piss on your territory if you do not piss on mine.' This means that meetings of the executive team are a bizarre ritual in which there are a series of duels between the CEO and each director. All the other directors get to watch the show until it is their turn for a duel with the CEO. Advice may be well meant, but it is treated as interference. In the executive suite that is called politics and nearly always results in retaliation.

The only help people value is the help they ask for. If they don't ask, don't give. It can be difficult to resist the temptation, especially if you see a team member struggling or going in the wrong direction. Let them learn: they will learn more from experience than from some unasked-for interference, however well-meaning it is. If they are too shy or too proud to ask for help, an innocent 'how's it going?' as you pass their desk should be enough to prompt the request.

Summary

Generosity is the art of taking by giving. It is not like being Father Christmas and distributing presents in the pursuit of popularity. Leaders do not need to be popular. They need to be trusted and respected. The search for popularity leads to weakness and a cycle of ever-growing expectations. Building trust builds commitment and loyalty, which are much less fickle than the demands of popularity.

> Leaders do not need to be popular. They need to be trusted

Generosity in the management world is about giving the most scarce resource of all. The most scarce resource in management is not money, it is time. Being generous with personal time appears to be suicidal when there are so many day-to-day pressures to meet. But by creating a network of alliances, mutual obligations and debts which can be called in, the influencer invests heavily in the future. It is an investment which saves time and raises performance in the longer term.

> The most scarce resource in management is not money, it is time

Ultimately, generosity is a habit. Fortunately, it is a habit that can be acquired. It is not just profitable to give, it is also enjoyable. And the meaner business becomes, the easier it is for the selfless and generous manager to stand out and become influential.

Part Three

Weave your web:
building commitment
and loyalty

Chapter 7

The partnership principle: become the trusted partner

Who would you rather work with: someone you trust or someone you do not trust? The answer is obvious. But how you develop trust is not obvious. If we are to become influential, we need to become the trusted partner of the people we influence. Achieving this goal is hard in a business context, because most business relationships start with the wrong script. There are typically three sorts of relationship in business:

- Boss to team member
- Team member to boss
- Colleague to colleague.

These relationships can be healthy or unhealthy. The unhealthy relationships often have the wrong underlying script:

- Boss to team member: Parent/child relationship. This can be nurturing and supportive. It can also be controlling and directive. The boss can use or abuse authority at will. Most of us have experience of both sorts of boss.
- Team member to boss. Child/parent relationship. The team member has no authority over the boss, and is highly dependent on the boss. It requires some ingenuity and adaptability to influence the boss effectively, even if the boss is benign.
- Colleague to colleague. This should be a productive adult-to-adult relationship. In practice it can be a rival-to-rival relationship or it is a beggar/donor relationship when one person needs something from another.

If we see people as bosses or rivals the whole time, then there is a natural tendency to feel fear and loathing respectively. Fear and loathing is not a great starting point for partnership. To get around all of this, organisations extol the virtues of teamwork and team players. If you happen to find yourself in a high-performing team, that is a wonderful experience. As individual managers, we cannot rely on being surrounded by committed and cooperative colleagues the whole time. We have to know how to create effective partnerships ourselves, without relying on the organisation to deliver those partnerships for us.

If we follow five principles we can move from being a boss, team member, rival or resource to being a trusted partner who carries influence and can make things happen:

1   Treat people as humans, not as roles

2   Act and look like a partner

3   Be credible

4   Be selfless

5   Make the most of moments of truth.

Treat people as humans, not roles

The starting point is surprisingly simple. We should recall the words of Julius Caesar's slave, who had the job of whispering in his ear 'Remember, you are only a human.' It is tempting to think of people as bosses, rivals or, worst of all, resources. They are all humans. To misquote Shylock in *The Merchant of Venice*:

I am a boss. Hath
not a boss eyes? Hath not a boss hands, organs,
dimensions, senses, affections, passions? Fed with
the same food, hurt with the same weapons, subject
to the same diseases, healed by the same means,
warmed and cooled by the same winter and summer, as

a colleague is? If you prick us, do we not bleed?
if you tickle us, do we not laugh? If you poison
us, do we not die? And if you wrong us, shall we not
revenge?

It can be very hard to think of a boss or a client as a human being. There are one or two bosses I have had whom I still have my doubts about. They were not entirely productive relationships. The bigger the boss, the more we see them as a role, not a person. Tony Blair, the former British prime minister, found it disconcerting to be addressed as 'Prime Minister.' He sometimes wondered whether he really existed as a person or simply as a title. The people who were closest to him and really influenced him called him Tony (in private) and treated him as a human being.

Organisations thrive on hierarchy and formality, even as they preach equality, informality and teamwork. To visit a headquarters is to be invited to a steel and glass monument to the success of the business. Corporate headquarters exude power and prestige. Behind the façade, the reality is of office politics and a constant struggle against the forces of chaos and entropy. The impressive impersonal façade gives way to the reality of human nature.

When you start treating people as humans, not roles, the nature of the relationship changes.

Act and look like a partner

We have already looked at the principles of acting and looking the part in Chapter 4. Remember that firms preach diversity but practise intimacy. Even if there is diversity of race, sex and faith, firms want people who share the same values, outlook and assumptions. Such people often share the same dress code and behaviour. Such conformity may not be healthy for the long-term survival of the firm, but it makes cooperation and mutual understanding much easier within the firm. Instead of fighting the system, we should influence the system. A good influencer will learn to wear the mask of conformity. You may be a weekend Hell's Angel with a motorbike, leathers and attitude to match. But during the week, it pays to know the code of influence and success.

Acting like a partner changes the way people work with you. For instance, I decided to start a bank. Previously, we saw how I managed to get a meeting with some bank CEOs. Normally, I feel justifiably nervous when my bank manager asks to see me. Seeing the CEO of the bank made me break out into a cold sweat. The bank seemed intent on inflicting architectural shock and awe on all customers, suppliers and rivals who approached them. It had a huge, impressive head office. The CEO had a special lift to the executive floor where the carpets were deeper and the flowers were fresher than anywhere else. There was an anteroom to the secretary's room where you were kept waiting like a schoolboy waiting to see the headmaster. So how do you now approach the CEO with your idea for a new bank?

The obvious answer is that you produce a well-arranged case and present it to him. Make sure you have all the detail worked out and make sure that every slide on your PowerPoint presentation is perfect. Rehearse your pitch so that you are also word perfect.

If you take the obvious route, you are not a partner with the CEO. You are yet another supplicant coming into his office pitching for some vested interest. CEOs are used to that script: they get to act as judge, jury and grand inquisitor all rolled into one. It is an adversarial relationship in which the CEO has all the power. The chances of success are small.

So I took an alternative route. I went in with no paper at all. I simply talked to him about his business, where the gaps and opportunities might lie and where the competition was weak or dangerous. It was a partnership discussion, which I had carefully prepared beforehand. I shared some of my dubious expertise with him, for his benefit, and he shared his prejudices with me. At the end, we agreed there was an opportunity. Several paperless meetings later, he asked me how much it would cost.

'About a billion,' I said.

'Dollars or pounds?' he asked.

'Pounds,' I quickly replied, deciding to give myself a few hundred million dollars more wiggle room.

And with that we had an informal agreement. We agreed that I would get his staff people to work up a formal proposal to conform to the arcane financial and accounting practices of his bank, and we would then present that to the board. We were acting as partners to chase a mutually attractive goal. If I had been a salesman trying to pitch a new business idea, I would have had a much harder time convincing a sceptical CEO and an even more sceptical planning and finance staff function.

PowerPoint is a badge of shame which junior staff and salespeople are often forced to wear. Partners do not convince each other over a PowerPoint presentation: they convince each other over a cup of coffee.

If you want to act and look the part, then see how peers really interact. Learn the code and use it to your advantage. If you act as a peer and a partner you will be treated as one. If you act as a nervous junior or a cocky salesman, you will get treated that way. To become the trusted partner, there are three more principles to work on.

Be credible

Credibility and trust go hand in hand. We may like people who look and act like us, but we will not trust them if they cannot deliver and they are not reliable. The implication is that credibility comes from actions, not words: it will build slowly and incrementally over time. In the long term, this is true. Deep partnerships come with deep credibility: both sides of the partnership understand their respective capabilities and have established long track records.

The challenge is how to build credibility and trust in the short term. If we want to influence someone, we cannot afford to wait five years while we build up a track record of success with that person. We need a shorthand way of building credibility fast.

The fastest way to claim credibility is to lay out your credentials. This is what every job seeker does with a CV. It can also make sense to send CVs in advance to prospective new clients, so that they have time to check you out in advance. It also avoids some brag fest trap which is described below. In day-to-day work, it is not natural to send your CV to colleagues, bosses or other firms. We need another way of achieving the same goal.

Watching two businesspeople meet for the first time is like watching two dogs sniffing each other. Each side wants to check the other, and wants to know who is the top dog. So the conversation turns quickly to who has done what and who has worked with whom. It is a brag fest: both sides are bragging, typically about their experience or their contacts. The problem with bragging is that what is said and what is heard are completely different. The speaker thinks he is setting out credentials, establishing credibility and trust.

The listener hears a competition in which the reactions are likely to be negative:

- If your experience is less than mine: why should I listen to you?
- If your experience is better than mine: I will show you that it is not relevant to me. Do not try to demean me.

There is another way of establishing credibility:

- Listen: Let them brag, let them talk about their triumphs, disasters and challenges. There is no need to compete with them. Learn about their situation, build rapport and show understanding.
- Ask smart questions: good questions show expertise and encourage more disclosure.
- Show some insight: once you have an understanding of the situation, then you can add some ideas and add some value. Instead of general bragging, you can focus your insight on the critical area of mutual interest. You show credibility by co-operating, not competing.
- Follow up: rapid follow-up is a quick way to build credibility. It can be as simple as sending a summary of the meeting, forwarding a relevant paper or link, or making an introduction. Do it fast and the recipient will be quietly impressed. Do it consistently after each meeting and you cement a positive reputation.

There is a trick to sharing expertise well. Done poorly, it can still sound like bragging. First, make sure that your expertise is focused on the immediate subject. For instance, in a contracts discussion a new colleague started talking about how he had been involved in many other contracts. It was pointless bragging which annoyed everyone else. Another colleague waited. When the discussion turned to the subject of guarantees, he calmly laid out a range of good and poor examples of contract guarantees. He established expertise and credibility through cooperation, not competition. He was the person we started to turn to. He had acquired influence which the bragger could only dream about.

Be selfless

It is very hard to trust anyone who appears to be in it for themself. In June 2009 the BBC published a survey in conjunction with

IPSOS/Mori. It found that 80 per cent of the public did not trust their elected MP to tell the truth. The reason for this appeared later in the survey: 84 per cent thought that MPs were in it for themselves or, occasionally, for their party. Only 11 per cent thought that MPs put the interests of their constituency or country first. If you appear selfish, it is very hard to be a trusted partner and it is hard to exert positive influence.

If you wish to appear selfless, it pays to act early. Once a reputation is established, it tends to stick. So make the first impressions count. The best way to appear selfless is to be selfless: offer to help your partner, even if it has some cost to yourself in the short term.

For instance, I have a builder. His name is 'sand and cement' Jim: there is no problem he has ever come across which cannot be sorted out with a little sand and cement. I keep him well clear of the electrics and plumbing. When I first met him, he hooked me with a simple act of apparent selflessness. We had agreed on a price for some work. Halfway through, he found another problem, which he fixed (with a little sand and cement) at no extra cost to me. It cost him little but earned him much. By not asking for more money he appeared trustworthy and put himself at the head of the pack for some much larger work which had to be done later.

Because business is becoming meaner and leaner, it is far easier to stand out with small acts of selflessness. A little investment goes far. If you look, you can always find ways of appearing selfless. Frequently, such selfless acts reap rich rewards. For instance, I went to see a client about a project review. He was frazzled and clearly not in the mood to talk about project reviews. So I asked him what was going on. He moaned about a big speech he had to give at an industry conference. He had hired a speech writer and the results were ugly: it was clever speech making, but it was not what the client wanted to say, or how he had wanted to say it. He was not a happy bunny! As it happened, I was used to writing speeches for politicians, so I said I could help him informally. It took an evening or so of personal time to craft the relevant speaking notes: I knew the client's industry and his personal style, so it was no great problem. The client was delighted and the speech went well. Mysteriously, we all got a major contract extension from him three months later.

An Asian client did not know how to go about getting his teenage children into university in Europe. That was an easy win: make an introduction to a professor who had interests in the client's area and let them carry on the conversation. The result was a happy professor, client, kids and consultant; it was a win-win-win.

If you look you can always find opportunities to shine through selfless acts: put in some discretionary effort, make an introduction, forward some relevant reading material. Inevitably, there will be freeloaders, who take you for granted and simply ask for more without giving anything in return. Don't whinge or whine about them. Quietly become unavailable or inaccessible for such people. Most people will feel the urge to reciprocate. If they are powerful, it will cost them personally nothing to make sure a promotion, good assignment or contract comes your way.

Make the most of moments of truth

Crises and conflicts make or break reputations, trust and partnerships. Moments of truth will be covered in full in Chapter 10. For now, it is enough to note the principles which enable a manager to build trust and credibility in what are often adverse circumstances. Turning adversity into advantage is essential in two sorts of situation:

- Crises
- Conflicts.

Crises happen. This is when people reveal the best and worst of their character. Some people simply hide. Others play the blame game. Others plunge into an orgy of analysis. None of these are very helpful reactions. In contrast, people who offer hope, provide a solution and drive to action are like gold dust. In the credit crunch there were hordes of commentators and politicians who were spreading blame and analysing. None of them came out of the crisis looking very good. The few who have come out with their reputations intact are those who have been positive, and focused on actions and solutions. Acting like this takes courage: it is safer to take refuge in analysis. To be truly influential requires taking some risk and standing out from the crowd rather than simply following it.

Conflict is natural within any organisation. Occasionally, the cold war of interdepartmental attrition can flare up into a nasty hot war. The temptation is to win the argument and leave the field victorious. There are some limited circumstances when it is right to fight (see Chapter 10). In principle, however, it is better to win a friend than win an argument. If you win the argument you earn an enemy: you have lost any positive influence or trust over that person. If you win a friend, it is much easier to settle any differences once you are past the immediate heat of the moment. By dealing with the conflict well, you will probably have strengthened your alliance and mutual respect.

Turning hostility into alliance is based on some simple principles:

- Focus on the outcome: where do you want to get to: a win–win or a win–lose? Is there a mutual goal that you can both rally around?
- Depersonalise the conflict: conflict can get very messy and personal. Do not rise to the bait. If there is blame to assign, blame the system not the person.
- Find common ground: move the debate areas of disagreement to areas of agreement. Build up from those.
- Buy time: focus on what you can do, not on what you cannot do. Time cools emotions and allows solutions to emerge.

Summary

Influential people are influential because they have a wide web of deep relationships. Over the years the number of crises and conflicts build up: each time you are either extending your web or weakening it. Use these occasions well to extend your web of influence. Other managers may want to win the odd battle: influence requires winning the war and building up your network of alliances and power.

Chapter 8

Build trust

Trust is the currency of influence. To understand how far we depend on trust, pick up a dollar bill. It is inscribed with the words 'In God We Trust'. Regardless of faith in religion, we need faith in money. We give the dollar bill to a shopkeeper, and we both accept that it is worth a dollar. We exchange another piece of green paper and we both trust that it is worth $20. Give the shopkeeper another piece of green paper and … it will be worth nothing if it is just a piece of green paper. Trust, even more than money, makes the world go round.

> Trust is the currency of influence

When trust disappears, disaster ensues. On 14 September 2007 huge queues appeared outside the branches of one of Britain's largest mortgage lenders: Northern Rock. Trust that the bank would be able to pay its depositors vanished overnight and suddenly all their customers wanted their money back. The bank quickly went under and had to be rescued by the government: it turned out to be the overture to the credit crunch.

Trust is so central to our lives that we take it for granted, like breathing air. Fortunately, most of us are reasonably trusting most of the time. If we distrusted money, banks, the safety of food, air travel and the water we drink, then life would become very hard. We also tend to trust each other, more or less. Twice as many people believe, as opposed to disbelieve, that the average person in the street is telling the truth. This is largely because there is no great reason for them to have to lie to us. Whether we trust them any further (like lending them $5 for a fare which they promise to mail back to us) is a moot point. In other words trust is not like an on/off switch where we either trust or do not trust someone. There are degrees of trust: trusting a stranger to tell the truth is about the weakest form of trust there is.

Trust is in the eye of the beholder. We may see ourselves as trustworthy, but that does not count. We have to be seen to be trustworthy by other people. Being in a position of authority does not automatically mean that we will be trusted. Some people in authority are trusted; others are not, as can be seen from public attitudes to different professions. The survey below asked a simple question: do you trust this profession to tell the truth?

Net 'tell the truth score' (US)	
Doctors	73%
Teachers	68%
Scientists	58%
Journalists	–19%
Trade union leaders	–30%
Lawyers	–41%

Source: Adapted from Harris Poll #61 2006

'Tell the truth score' = % trust profession to tell truth less % not trust profession to tell truth.

It is as well that we trust doctors and teachers, and perhaps not surprising that we do not trust lawyers, union leaders and journalists. Politicians and stockbrokers also did very poorly, and that was before the credit crunch massacred the reputation of financial services professionals. These findings are remarkably consistent across borders. A similar (not identical) survey in the UK also put doctors and teachers as the most trusted professionals. Journalists were once again near the bottom, along with politicians and business leaders.

Net 'tell the truth score' (UK)	
Doctors	86%
Teachers	79%
Professors	70%
Business leaders	−29%
Politicians	−52%
Journalists	−55%

Source: Ipsos/MORI Veracity Index 2008.

Within the workplace, trust is essential. Policy manuals and company directives cannot legislate for trust. The most influential managers tend to be the most trusted: people are prepared to work with people they trust, not with people they do not trust.

Trust has to be earned, not claimed. A short example shows how untrustworthy we sound when we claim to be trustworthy: 'Look, OK, John, I'm a straight sort of guy ... Of course I'm an honest sort of a bloke – If I were lying... ' (Prime Minister Tony Blair, BBC Radio 4, 13 May 2005, on the Iraq report). Once you start proclaiming your honesty and trustworthiness you start to sound like a con merchant or, worse, a politician.

Trust is not some elusive pixie dust that some managers have and others lack. It is something every practising manager can acquire, with effort. Trust is the function of four variables, which we can arrange as a simple equation. Here it is in all its spurious mathematical accuracy:

$T = (VxC)/(RxD)$

Where:

T = trust

V = Values alignment

C = Credibility

R = Risk

D = Distance.

To understand how to build trust we need to know how to manage each of the four variables. As we start, remember that trust is built one person at a time.

Values alignment

The more that we appear to share common values, outlooks and priorities with someone else, the more we are likely to trust them. This can be as much social as business alignment. If two people share similar backgrounds, faith, political outlook, education or experiences then they are more likely to trust each other. We may preach the values of diversity, but we prefer conformity. Diversity means challenge and is good both for society and for business. But day to day, managers prefer to work with people with whom there is the minimum chance of misunderstanding. The glaring lack of diversity at the top of most companies is the product of this conformity bias. To the extent that women get into the boardroom, it is mainly to make tea. Under 15 per cent of board directors in the UK and USA are women, and the majority of those are in non-executive positions. Equally, if you look at the top of French, Chinese, American, or Japanese companies, they tend to be run by home-country nationals. The exceptions are notable, but not typical. The overwhelming evidence is that managers prefer conformity to diversity.

This simple observation drives much behaviour. For instance, I was invited to go shooting in the north of England. This was not an invitation to join an urban gang and get into a drugs war. It was an invitation to shoot some grouse on a moor. I accepted, which was a mistake on nearly every level. Guns scare me, and gun owners scare me even more. But the event was a great success, for most of the party of businessmen. They were lousy shots, which was good for the grouse. But anyone who wants to go to an event like that shares a certain world outlook: highly traditional and very right-wing. So they spent the whole weekend confirming to each other that the world was in a terrible state and it needed decent people like themselves to put it right again. By the end of the weekend, they had achieved perfect values alignment with each other. They were ready to do plenty of business deals with each other because they found trust in each other.

Shooting in the office is probably not the best way to build values alignment. Fortunately, there are simpler ways of doing this.

The first step in building values alignment is to listen. The art of listening has already been covered in some detail. Listening sympathetically allows the speaker to believe that you respect their world view. It also allows you to discover what that world view is. Even if there is much you dislike or disagree with, you should be able to find some areas of common ground. Focus the conversation on areas of agreement, not disagreement. Even if the only area of agreement is about your favourite films or sports, that is a step in the right direction.

We cannot pretend to have the same values as everyone else. But we can at least respect other people's values. Showing interest, and even admiration, for someone else's values, choices and lifestyle helps to build trust. Respect shows that you are not going to attack or belittle someone for who they are and what they do. And there is always something good to find in anyone. For instance, working with one politician I found he always had a good word to say for everyone he met. I watched as he was introduced to a stranger:

Politician: 'So what do you do?'

Stranger: 'I am a pawnbroker.'

I laughed inwardly. What on earth could the politician say to that? Pawnbrokers in popular mythology prey upon the weakest and most vulnerable, making money at their expense. Surely there is not much good to say there.

Politician: 'Magnificent! Pawnbrokers were the very first bankers: they started commerce as we know it. And now you provide a vital service to all those people who cannot get credit anywhere else....'

As the politician spoke, I saw the pawnbroker puff himself up with pride. He had found someone who understood him and respected him. That was another vote in the bag for the politician.

If you can share the same values, or show respect for other people's values, you have made a start in building trust.

Credibility

If you can 'talk the talk' (values alignment) you also have to 'walk the walk' (credibility). You must be able to do as you say. Credibility is as fragile as a vase:

> Credibility is as fragile as a vase: one slip and it is broken for good

one slip and it is broken for good. In Shakespeare's words: 'Trust not the person who has broken faith once.'

If we are to maintain our credibility, we have to manage expectations very carefully. It is easy to make promises without realising that we have made a promise. When the expectation is not fulfilled, we have failed even although we think we have done nothing wrong. Much of this comes down to the use of language. For instance, we may say things like:

'I will try to...'

'I hope to....'

'I will do my best....'

Clearly, we think we are not making a commitment. These are weasel words which politicians use. They give us a get-out clause if things don't turn out right. But what we say and what is heard are different things. What is heard is 'I will....'. When we have tried, hoped and done our best but not been able to deliver, we have just failed to live up to a perceived commitment. We have to make sure we set the right perceptions and expectations. If we are not sure that we can do something we need to be clearer: weasel words are not enough. We have to spell out precisely why something may not be possible and when we will find out whether we really can do it or not.

Even when we say nothing, we can lose credibility. Annual reviews are a critical moment when bosses build or lose trust with their team. Team members can take bad news, but they find it hard to accept surprises. If you have kept quiet, or been evasive about a team member's weaknesses, you will find the annual review will be problematic. If you suddenly discover honesty in the annual review, the reviewee will be in shock and denial. If you have been honest throughout the year, given clear feedback and support, then you will have managed expectations well: bad news will not be a surprise. Being honest throughout the year builds credibility and respect. Team members hate ambiguity and uncertainty. Being clear about performance allows them to improve in good time.

The process of building credibility is slow. If we believe the average person in the street, it is because we have not had the chance to be let down by them. Going from that weak form of trust to a strong form of trust takes time. In practice, we have countless opportunities to prove our credibility and trustworthiness. After a first meeting we can send a quick summary, or a thank you note, or follow up on an action point on the same day.

> If we believe the average person in the street, it is because we have not had the chance to be let down by them

By doing so, we put down a marker that we can be trusted. If someone leaves a message for us, we build credibility by replying fast. If we have to be reminded to reply, or if we have to be reminded about an action point, we lose credibility. From these very small beginnings, we can move on to larger demonstrations of credibility.

The higher the stakes, the more important it is to manage expectations and to deliver on our promises. For team members, promises of promotions, assignments and bonuses are very high stakes. And humans being humans, we tend to hear what we want to hear. We want to hear that we are going to get the best assignment, the next promotion and the best bonus: we will certainly believe that we deserve it. Against these expectations, managers have to be brutally honest and clear. It feels awkward to be so clear and honest, but it is a far better way of building respect and credibility than disappearing into the jungle of vague words and half-promises.

Credibility and values intimacy drive trust up over time. There are also two things which drive trust down: risk and distance. We have to manage these as actively as we manage our credibility and demonstrate our values.

Risk

Risk is the rust in trust. It is corrosive of our ability to trust people. The higher the risk, the less inclined we are to trust strangers. In the veracity surveys above we saw that most of us will trust strangers to tell the truth.

> Risk is the rust in trust

Unless we wish to achieve great poverty, we are unlikely to trust a stranger with our life savings.

Within the workplace there are two ways we can use risk to advantage. We can reduce it or raise it.

A good way to manage risk is to raise it, selectively. If a new course of action looks risky, people will naturally prefer to do nothing. The response may be to reduce the perceived risk of the new idea. Equally valid is to raise the perceived risk of doing nothing. When doing nothing looks extremely risky, people start looking for alternatives. If

> A good way to manage risk is to raise it

necessary, create the crisis and focus people on its dire

consequences. This is what the president of a global electronics firm did to great effect. The firm was in crisis, under the onslaught of Asian competition. To survive, the firm needed a major cost-cutting drive. The president issued a simple message: 20 per cent off costs, 20 per cent off working capital, 20 per cent off headcount by year end.

The first reaction was that all the division heads identified all the logical risks and reasons why the goals were unachievable. For instance:

- We have just cut by 20 per cent so surely we cannot cut again

- We are growing by 20 per cent so that means we should not have to make any cuts

- We already have the best benchmark costs in the industry, so we should not cut

- We are R&D/marketing/sales and the future of the company, so you cannot cut us.

when you accept excuses, you accept failure

These were all rational and logical objections. If the president had accepted them, the firm would now be bankrupt: when you accept excuses, you accept failure. The risks and problems that the division heads identified were rational and logical, but would have led the firm to bankruptcy.

The president decided to increase the stakes and raise the risk of doing nothing. To his list of 20 per cent cuts he added one more cut for the division heads to think about: 'if you do not deliver the 20 per cent cut, you will be part of the 20 per cent'. Suddenly, the risk of doing nothing soared compared to the risk of taking on the 20 per cent. More widely, he made it clear that the choice was not between 20 per cent cuts or no cuts. It was between 20 per cent cuts and 100 per cent cuts from bankruptcy.

Cutting 20 per cent of staff sounds terrible. But going bankrupt (the banks wanted their money back) and getting wiped out by foreign competition was even worse. If the choice was losing 20 per cent of jobs or no job losses, everyone would have stayed with the status quo. When the choice was to lose 20 per cent of jobs or 100 per cent of jobs, the 20 per cent option started to look a lot more attractive.

Most organisations and managers resist change because change is riskier than doing nothing. Increasing the perceived risk of doing nothing alters that equation in favour of change.

The more conventional way of managing the perception of risk is to reduce it. The key is to understand that risk is not just logical: it is emotional and personal. Project managers who fall in love with their risk and issue logs miss the point. Their logical risks can be managed away with appropriate remedial actions. The killer risks are personal:

- How will this idea affect me and my prospects?
- How much effort will I have to put in?
- How will I look if this idea succeeds or fails?

When colleagues object to an idea they will use rational objections, because managers have to pretend to be rational. This is what the president's division heads did: they used rational objections to try to stop something which they personally did not like. This opens up a huge bear trap for

> Fighting emotional objections with logical answers is like fighting fire with fuel

managers. Fighting emotional objections with logical answers is like fighting fire with fuel: it normally ends in tears.

The influential manager will learn to separate out rational from emotional responses. Truly logical risks have a pattern all of their own:

- They will not be a surprise: the more creative and unexpected the challenge, the more likely it is to be a rational objection hiding an emotional fear
- They will be presented positively: 'how do we deal with'....rather than 'it's impossible because...'
- They lead to a discussion of solutions
- They come in small doses, rather than vast hordes of objections.

Logical risks can be dealt with logically. Emotional risks need to be dealt with emotionally. The electronics president had an effective way of doing this: raise the stakes personally for each division head. In less traumatic times it pays to reduce the perceived risks. This is a combination of listening (Chapter 5) and the art of the persuasive conversation (Chapter 12). These are discussions which are only productive in private. In public, managers have to maintain the rational façade. In private, they can be more open about their personal interests and agenda.

Distance

Distance is the opposite of values intimacy and credibility. The greater the distance between two people, the less likely they are to trust each other. There are four main types of distance:

- Distance between what we say and what we mean
- Distance between what we say and what we do
- Distance between your interests and my interests
- Distance between my background, experience and values and yours.

What we say and what we mean

To understand the distance between what we say and what we mean, listen to a politician. They are masters at using language to say one thing and mean something else. For instance, in the

Monica Lewinsky affair, President Clinton said there was no sexual relationship. If you use a very narrow definition of 'sexual relationship' he was right. But he was also misleading. And when politicians are caught misleading, they will not admit it. They will use phrases such as 'I mis-spoke' or 'terminological inexactitude' for a lie. Then they wonder why they are not trusted.

George Orwell predicted the rise of double speak in his novel *1984*, where ministries did the opposite of what they were labelled, for instance:

- Ministry of Peace: responsible for continuous war
- Ministry of Plenty: responsible for rationing
- Ministry of Truth: responsible for propaganda
- Ministry of Love: responsible for suppression and torture of dissidents.

The business world is quickly following the political world, using words to avoid saying it straight. The 12 most dangerous, and misleading words in business are:

1   *Just*: This is used to make a huge request or error seem trivial as in: 'Could you just do this (500 page) document by Monday?' It is a request best made late on a Friday afternoon.

2   *But*: Remember, whatever is said before 'but' is baloney, as in, 'That was a great presentation, but...', or 'I would like to help, but...'.

3   *From*: Much loved by advertisers, as in 'Fly to Rome from £10', excluding £100 of taxes and other 'optional' extras for a flight leaving at 4 am, going to an airport about 100km away from Rome and the ticket has to be booked one year in advance.

4   *Might* (and any other conditional verb): 'Might' is used to achieve two things: first it sets up a negotiating position as in, 'I might be able to do that if...'. Second, it lays the groundwork for excusing failure later on: 'I would have done it, if only...' .

5 *Only*: Closely related to 'Just', it is an attempt to make a big request or problem seem small. 'It was only a small error … we only dropped one nuclear bomb over London…'.

6 *Important* (and urgent): Used to puff up any presentation: 'This important new product/initiative…'. Important to whom? And why? Maybe it is important to the speaker, but why is it to me?

7 *Strategic*: 'Important', with bells on. See Strategic Human Capital division, formerly known as the Personnel Department. Alternatively used to justfiy something which has no financial justification at all: 'This strategic IT investment … (which costs £100 million and has no identifiable payback at all) is essential to the survival of the business'.

8 *Rightsize, downsize, best shore, offshore, outsource, optimise, redeploy, downshift, re-engineer*: How many ways are there of avoiding saying straight up: 'we are going to lay off staff'?

9 *Thank you*: Normally 'Thank you' is good, except when used by automated voices at call centres saying, 'Thank you for calling, we value your call … (and we have so much contempt for our customers that we cannot be bothered to answer your call promptly, so we will put you on hold until you give up and try to use our impenetrable and useless online help instead)'.

10 *Interesting*: Fear this word. When your lawyer uses it, you are doomed. When your doctor uses it, check your will is up to date. The recession is certainly interesting. A slightly less interesting time would be preferable.

11 *Opportunity*: Because the word 'problem' has been banned in business speak, all problems have become opportunities. This means many opportunities are problems. There is a limit to how many opportunities I can solve. Interesting and strategic opportunities really scare me.

> Interesting and strategic opportunities really scare me

12 *Investment*: 'Investment' was first hijacked by the British government to justify wild and uncontrolled public sector spending. Spending is bad, but investment is good, so they simply reclassify spending as investment and make the bad sound good.

There is some good news in this. The more jargon and weasel words become endemic, the less managers are trusted. This creates space for managers who use plain words and say what they mean to stand out from the rest of the pack. Sometimes, the art of influence is not too sophisticated. Do the basics right and you can be noticeably different and better than colleagues who try to be clever.

The distance between what we say and what we do

Most of us do not set out to be dishonest. But we can inadvertently set expectations which we cannot meet, as shown in the section on credibility above. The problem is not what we say: it is what our colleagues decide to hear. If in doubt, overcommunicate. Steve, who ran a life insurance firm, developed the rule of five to cope with this problem: 'do not think anyone has understood anything until they have heard it at least five times'. His rationale for the rule of five was:

● First time: statement not heard amid the noise of other messages
● Second time: statement heard but ignored
● Third time: statement heard but not really believed
● Fourth time: statement heard, believed and misunderstood
● Fifth time: they might have got it.

Besides repetition, consistency and accuracy are essential. Assume that people hear what they want to hear: they will misinterpret what you say to minimise the downside and maximise the upside. If you say something five times, they will hear whichever version they want to hear. If you are consistent, there is only one message they can hear.

The distance between my interests and your interests

The distance between your interests is the opposite of values intimacy. Eighty per cent of survey respondents (BBC Ipsos/MORI 2009) believe that politicians act mainly in their interests or the interests of their party: few believe they act in the interests of the country or their constituents. Equally, the scandals over excessive CEO pay make many fear that CEOs are acting mainly in their own interests, not in the interests of staff or shareholders. Business leaders and politicians rank low on perceived veracity.

To close the gap we need to act with selfless independence, at least occasionally. We need to show that we understand, respect and if necessary adapt to the needs of other people. If all we ever do is chase our own interests, then few people will feel the need to trust us.

Organisations are designed around competing and conflicting interests (see Chapter 10: Pick your battles). Each function and department has a different set of priorities and perspectives. As we shall see later, influencers learn to collaborate rather than compete across the firm.

The distance between my background and yours

A consistent theme throughout *How to Influence* is the desire for intimacy and conformity. We find it far easier to deal with people like ourselves, because we think we understand such people. Diversity sounds good in politicians' speeches, but even they do not practise it. The vast majority choose to live in single-race marriages: daytime diversity leads to sunset segregation.

Even in firms with a strongly conformist culture, different people are...different. Age alone is a great divider in everything from personal priorities, experience and taste in music. Asking a 60-year-old and a 20-year-old to listen to each other's music is normally a recipe for pain and disbelief.

The easiest way to reduce the background gap is to listen (Chapter 5). Even if you do not share their world view, by listening you show you respect them. You also learn about them and can find a few areas in common: build on what is common, not on what is different.

Summary

Trust is the invisible force behind the invisible hand of influence. It has to be invisible. The more you talk about trust openly, the less trustworthy you seem: you will sound like a politician. Some people carry an aura of trust around with them; others do not. But there is no mystery to this aura. Building and using trust comes down to the simple trust equation:

$T = (VxC)/(RxD)$

The mathematics may not be sound but the logic is: values intimacy and credibility build trust; risk and distance weaken trust. It is an equation which can be used to build the most productive relationships of all: the high-trust partnerships.

Chapter 9

Play the
right tune

Ever since Freud created psychoanalysis, therapists have been trying to work out how people work. How much progress they have made is open to debate. Most of us do not have the time, expertise or need to become psychoanalysts. We need some shorthand methods of quickly understanding and influencing our friends and colleagues.

Fortunately, we do not need to put our colleagues on the couch to understand them. To get onto their wavelength, there are two things we can do.

- Write the right script
- Tune into our colleagues: adapt to their style.

For each of these goals, there is a simple tool we can use to help ourselves.

Write the right script

I recently became a trillionaire, many times over. In real hard cash. I reckon I have $400,000,000,000,000. I may be out by the odd billion, but in truth we trillionaires are not too bothered by a few billion dollars here or there. I have the money in my pocket. Unfortunately, the dollars are Zimbabwean dollars and my four $100-trillion notes are not enough to buy me a bus fare in Zimbabwe, the land of the world's starving billionaires.

Gideon Gono has been the governor of the Central Bank of Zimbabwe since 2003. In that time, Zimbabwe has slid from being the prosperous bread basket of Africa to hyperinflation, mass unemployment and dependency on food aid. As the top central banker of a Zimbabwe what sort of story do you construct for yourself?

a) I have been a complete idiot who has destroyed a prosperous country through a combination of greed, corruption and incompetence or

b) I have brilliantly withstood hostile foreign sanctions and introduced innovative policies which the rest of the world now follows, which shows that God is on my side.

You would probably construct a positive story about yourself. This is what Gideon Gono has done. Here is what he said to *Newsweek* in January 2009: 'I found myself doing extraordinary things that aren't in the textbooks. Then the IMF asked the U.S. to please print money. I began to see the whole world now in a mode of practicing what they have been saying I should not. I decided that God had been on my side and had come to vindicate me.'

Now think about who he listens to and who influences him. Will it be people who challenge his world view and tell him he is an idiot, or will it be people who support his world view? The chances are that he listens to people who understand and respect his script. If you want to understand people, understand their personal script or self-image. Everyone has a personal script, and they tend to be positive scripts.

As a test, rate yourself on the following activities as either below or above average relative to the rest of humanity: honesty, reliability, trustworthiness, driving, working and loving. Typically, 90 per cent of people think they are above average. This is statistically impossible, but emotionally inevitable. This picture is reflected in the annual assessment ritual. In many firms, 90 per cent of people are rated as average or above. The remaining 10 per cent either move on, shape up or get fired. It is human nature to think well of ourselves.

> 90 per cent of people think they are above average. This is statistically impossible, but emotionally inevitable.

Once you understand people's self-image, you can make them do more or less anything provided it reinforces that self-image. For instance, one boss had me worked out completely. He knew I was an adventurer: I loved challenge and excitement. My boss also had a problem. The Japan business was not so much the land of the rising sun: it was more the land of the sinking business. It was a bottomless pit of endless losses. He needed someone to turn it around. My boss gave me a five-minute pitch about the excitement, exotic adventure and challenge of Japan and I was hooked. There were some minor problems: I spoke no Japanese, had never been to Japan and was completely unqualified for the task. And I was offered only a one-way ticket: that made it even more exciting. If I had thought about it, I would have turned it down: but logic was overwhelmed by emotion. Not going would be a denial of how

I saw myself and who I was: it was impossible for me not to accept the lousy challenge for the next three years of my life.

It takes time and effort to decode other people. But once you have made the investment, it keeps on paying dividends. Understanding people's self-image is the key to decoding people.

We all have an image of who we are. It may or may not be how other people see us. Our self-image can often be captured in a simple story about who we are and how we relate to the rest of the world. Inevitably, every story is unique because each human is unique. But in the workplace we can spot some common stories about how people like to see themselves. Listed below are 10 of the most common archetypes that you can see at work. As you skim through the list, you will probably find a few of your colleagues who fit some of these archetypes. Other colleagues may be a combination of archetypes, or you may be able to create your own script for them.

Once you understand how colleagues see themselves, you can work out three more things:

- How to use them: what value they bring
- How not to use them: where they are a liability
- How to influence them sustainably.

For each of the archetypes below, there is a very brief sketch of each of these three things.

Winner

Script: 'I win at *everything*: jobs, love, money, driving, sport, investing.'

Style: highly competitive, driven to overachieve, high need for control.

Value: Point them at the right windmill and they will charge.

Downside: Divisive. Poor in adversity: delusional and often self-destructive

Influencing key: Show you are also a winner, in another area. Do not compete directly, but do not be submissive: winners like to work with non-competing winners.

Angel

Script: 'I am an island of compassion and help in a cruel and heartless world.'

Style: Caring, nurturing and supportive.

Value: Can be a calming and unifying force in adverse ircumstances.

Downside: More focused on dealing with people than dealing with tasks.

Influencing key: Be empathetic, admire their work and ask for their help. They will like nurturing you.

Craftsman

Script: 'I am highly professional and skilled in my chosen trade.'

Style: Highly rational and analytical: not great on tasks or people.

Value: Often good at what they do.

Downside: rarely make good managers; tend to be insular and focused on their own job.

Influencing key: Respect, recognise their expertise: do not question their talent. Contradiction often works: 'this looks impossible, I was told no one in your department can do this… ' They will then prove you wrong by doing the impossible, thank you.

Puritan

Script: 'I am an island of decency in an ocean of immorality and idleness.'

Style: Decency, honesty, fair play, hard work.

Value: Often reliable team members who will work hard and quietly to deliver.

Downside: Don't invite them to your party, and don't mention your latest expenses claim.

Influencing key: Listen and let them moralise. Empathise with them. Recognise their work and their values, which may well be overlooked by other people.

Aristocrat

Script: 'I am socially superior and very well connected: should I talk to you?'

Style: Highly aware of people and status.

Value: Often well connected within and beyond the firm: can open doors.

Influencing key: Very pliable if you can offer them access to prestigious events and people. They want the bragging rights. Make them sweat: do not give them what they want immediately.

Bureaucrat

Script: 'I am diligent, effective and largely unrecognised.'

Style: Guided by the twin stars of fairness and efficiency, on a good day.

Value: Reliable, especially for administrative tasks.

Downside: Focus on process, not outcomes. Slow, uncreative, risk averse. May think management is about procedures, not people.

Influencing key: Show respect, comply with rules, procedures: avoid risk. Be clear and detailed about what you need from them.

Hero

Script: 'I save the world/firm/project from imminent disaster.'

Value: Often good in crises and with tight deadlines. Will make things happen.

Downside: Can be drama queens.

Influence key: Respect, admire their role in saving the world. Show you need them to save the world again in your area, and that this time the world will recognise it and be grateful.

Policeman

Script: 'My job is to stop disaster happening: I am the sheriff who controls all the cowboys around here.'

Value: Can identify and avoid risk: may be found in legal, health and safety, audit, brand police, etc.

Downside: Brains hard-wired to say 'no'.

Influence key: Involve them early. This shows them respect and means that their comments can be incorporated early and painlessly. Leave it late and you have an expensive political struggle.

Intellectual

Script: 'I am smarter than the fools who are my bosses and colleagues.'

Value: Driven by intellectual challenges.

Downside: Not good at people; can be a loner.

Influence key: Recognise their brilliance, ask for their advice, wisdom and experience. Give them a platform to display their talent.

Victim

Script: 'I suffer the slings and arrows of outrageous fortune with courage and fortitude. Poor me.'

Value: Not much. Believes events control them, rather than them controlling events.

Downside: Achieves little; drain on enthusiasm; passive victim.

Influence key: Best to avoid. If necessary, listen and empathise.

There are four common themes in dealing with all of these scripts:

- Listen to people: let them talk about themselves. That is how you will discover their script or self-image. You will be learning the tune to play to them.

- Respect their world view, empathise but do not try to compete with them. Do not try to be a better winner/victim/craftsman than the person you are talking to. They want to be exceptional. Do not challenge or threaten their world view: they will become highly defensive. Let them live with their own version of reality, even if you do not believe their nonsense. Your job is not to challenge or change their world view. You need to influence them, which means working with them, not against them.

- Recognise them. Very few people think that they are over-recognised. Most of us suspect that our talents and achievements are not adequately recognised in the wider world. Use this to your advantage. Recognise them in private, of course. But you may be able to go further. Perhaps you can stage an opportunity at an offsite meeting, at a presentation, at a dinner or awards event where they can be showcased.

- Money is not the main motivator. Money recognises their value relative to their colleagues. Even $1 million is an insult if their colleague is given more. As a colleague, you probably do not control their pay anyway, so you can focus on other influencing tools. Remember, no one denies who they are: if your idea or request reinforces their self-image, they will find it extremely hard to deny your request.

Two examples will show how you can use people's scripts to influence:

Amy was terrified at the prospect of presenting to the board, who were at least three levels above her. She did not know any of them and feared it would make or break her career. She did not want to do it. Outside work, Amy was a different character. She was an enthusiastic member of several community groups including a theatre group. She had given herself two scripts: at work she was the junior manager still learning her trade and working in the backroom of the business. In her social life she was the organiser and performer who liked to be centre stage. She needed to move her social script to work. So she was offered some presentation training, which would be run by an actor. The simple message was that all presentations are a performance: acting helps presenting. The presentation training would also help her acting. Eventually she went to the board, but she did not present: she performed for the board and performed brilliantly.

Dan was very clever and very cynical. He was the classic techno-crat: brilliant with his statistics but pretty much unable to relate to other human beings. He had a fairly dysfunctional script where he was the unrecognised and undervalued expert who knew all the answers, but no one was prepared to listen. He could do outstanding analysis, but he could also do highly destructive analysis: he could demolish more or less any spreadsheet or financial analysis which was presented to him.

For a big proposal, we knew we needed him on side because top management would use him to screen our proposal. The normal script would involve us having a long and bloody battle with him, interspersed with occasional pleas for a truce. Instead, we decided not to present the proposal to him. We went and listened to him and heard about the projects he was working on. We picked one which sounded relevant and made ourselves enthusiastic about it. We said that his work was so interesting, could he present a paper on it at our annual conference? We told him more people needed to hear about his work. Dan was delighted. At last he was getting recognition for his work; he was being given a platform to display his skills. It would be extra work, but it was well worth it.

Later, we went along and asked for some more help. Finally, we told him we needed some help on a proposal for top management. Dan the clever cynic suddenly became Dan the enthusiastic supporter. He showed us how our proposal was deeply flawed (he could have torn it to shreds) and then went on to show how we could make it bulletproof. We had taken the simple step of recognising and valuing an under-recognised and undervalued technocrat. So instead of fighting against us, he started fighting for us.

The dark side and the bright side of the script

There is a dark side to working the script. It can be highly manipulative and potentially destructive. At an extreme, the 'martyrdom' videos of suicide bombers show that they have completely bought into a script which tells them that the best thing a human can do is to kill other humans randomly. All dictators have scripts that tell them what they are doing is good. Often they assume that they do not represent the nation: they *are* the nation. If they are the nation, then all opposition is by definition sedition and treachery, and also all of the resources of the nation belong to them: wealth, power and corruption all go hand in hand.

At a more mundane level, British Members of Parliament have been found fleecing the taxpayer for personal gain: they have been putting everything on expenses from the cost of having their moat cleared to buying a floating duck house. And it is not one or two politicians who have had their snouts in the trough: it looks as though the majority have been in the swill. These are not obviously corrupt people. For the most part, they got into politics to change the world, not to buy a duck house. So what went wrong? Collectively they wrote the wrong script, which goes something like this:

'Every day we meet rich and powerful people. We work harder than most of them and are more deserving, but our salaries are small compared with those of the people we meet. Public opinion will not let us pay ourselves more, but we can make it up through the expenses system. As long as we stick within the rules (script) we have set for ourselves, then the expenses are a discreet way of making up our salaries.'

This script was self-reinforcing. When some politicians started following the script, initially without criticism, it showed that the script was a good one. Other politicians followed until it became standard practice. Internally, their script made perfect sense to themselves, until the details were exposed to public scrutiny. Then it looked like total folly and an abuse of taxpayers' money and trust.

When someone's script goes wrong, the consequences are ugly. Zinedine Zidane, captain of the French football team, was playing in the World Cup final, a match watched by over a billion people. Zidane was already a winner: he had won the World Cup before. He had a winner's script in his head. This was going to be his moment when he led his country once again to inevitable victory over Italy, their opposition. Unfortunately, the script started to go wrong. Italy were winning and time was running out. Someone had stolen his script. He was not a winner any more. If he was not a winner, he was nothing: he had no other script. He was not just losing a match, he was losing everything he stood for and his whole self-image. With a little Italian provocation, Zidane lost the plot completely and head-butted an opponent. He was sent off, France were down to 10 men and were condemned to defeat by his moment of madness.

As with all forms of power, influence can be put to good use or poor use. Influence is amoral: it makes no value judgements about what is right or wrong. Used well, scripts cannot only help influence other people: we can also help ourselves by writing the right script for ourselves.

> Influence is amoral: it makes no value judgements about what is right or wrong

A few examples will show how we can change our life chances by changing our script.

Teach First puts outstanding teachers into challenging schools. Many of the kids who attend these schools inherit very low aspirations from their parents. Living in the suburbs, they may never have been into the city and their life horizons are limited. Their script is of low ambition and has negative expectations. One Teach First initiative took 100 such children on visits to universities. By raising expectations and showing them what was possible, the children began to change their life script. The future was no longer about joining a gang or working in the local supermarket. They saw what was possible with hard work. Ninety per cent of them went on to university, and several of them went to elite universities.

Professor Richard Wiseman, in his book *The Luck Factor*, shows what makes people lucky. Part of it is that they make their own luck. The other part of it is that they create an internal script in which they see themselves as lucky. As a result they tend to recall all the moments when they got lucky. Unlucky people recall all the times they got unlucky. On the same trip, the lucky driver will recall all the times the lights changed in his favour. His unlucky passenger sitting next to him will recall all the times the lights changed against them. The same experience can be lucky or unlucky depending on the script you choose.

> What's your script, and what do you want it to be?

If we use scripts well, we cannot only influence others positively, we can also influence our own life. What's your script, and what do you want it to be?

Understanding and adapting to the style of our colleagues

> people should not be put in boxes until they are dead

There is a whole cottage industry devoted to understanding the styles of different people. For the most part, this involves categorising people and putting them in neat little boxes: people should not be put in boxes until they are dead.

Perhaps the most famous of these systems is MB/TI (the Myers-Briggs Type Indicators). MB/TI offers a series of style or type trade-offs. You can be:

- Extrovert or Introvert (E or I)
- Sensing or Intuitive (S or N)
- Thinking or Feeling (T or F)
- Judging or Perceiving (J or P).

MB/TI assigns each person a style and an acronym such as ESTJ or INFP. It provides insight, but it is difficult to learn and harder to apply. A short, revisionist and unauthorised version of how MB/TI works is shown below:

A revisionist version of MB/TI			
Type	Description	Positive impact	Negative impact
Extroversion (E)	Gains energy from others Speaks then thinks	Spreads energy, enthusiasm	Loud mouth, does not include other people.
Introversion (I)	Gains energy from within, thinks before speaks	Thoughtful, gives space to others	Nothing worth saying? Uneasy networker
Sensing (S)	Observes outside world More facts, less ideas	Practical, concrete, detailed	Dull, unimaginative
Intuitive (N)	Pays attention to self, inner world, idea	Creative, imaginative	Flighty, impractical, unrealistic
Thinking (T)	Decides with the head and logic	Logical, rational, intellectual	Cold and heartless
Feeling (F)	Listens to the heart	Empathetic, understanding	Soft-headed, fizzy thinker, bleeding heart

Type	Description	Positive impact	Negative impact
Judging (J)	Organised, scheduled, tidy	High work ethic, focused and reliable	Compulsive neat freak Upright, rigid, rule bound
Perceiving (P)	Keeps options open, opportunistic	Work–life balance, enjoys work	Lazy, messy, aimless and unreliable

As you look at the positive impact of each style, you are only human if you assume you have all the positive qualities. In practice, you are meant to be either extrovert or introvert, sensing or intuitive, thinking or feeling, judging or perceiving. You have to choose between the styles. A quicker way to make your choice is to look at the negative impacts of each style. This allows you to identify your own style and that of your partner relatively fast. If you spend a day or two in seminars about MB/TI (or any of the other style tools) you will discover their richness and depth. It takes months to become an expert practitioner. This defeats the object of the exercise: we do not want to become psychology experts. We need some simple shorthand for understanding and influencing our colleagues.

There are many other personality tests out there. All claim to be better than the others. Quite a few are available on the web, if you want to while away an odd hour getting to know who you are. To use them, most of these tools require months or even years of training, and they also often require detailed analysis of each of your colleagues. Managers do not have time to become psycho-analysts, nor do they have the time to analyse each of their colleagues in detail. We need something simpler, and quicker: welcome to the style compass, described below.

The easiest way to start is to think about how the person you want to influence operates. Forget the psychological mumbo-jumbo.

Just focus on the sorts of behaviour that you see most consistently. There are all sorts of possible trade-offs and behaviours you could identify. Here are a few to start with:

- Big picture vs. Detail
- Email vs. Face to face
- Task focus vs. People focus
- Open vs. Defensive
- Controlling vs. Empowering
- Analysing vs. Action
- Risk-taking vs Risk-avoiding
- Outcomes vs. Process
- Inductive vs. Deductive
- Prompt vs. Tardy
- Quick vs. Slow
- Positive vs. Cynical
- Judging vs. Sensing
- Rash vs. Contemplative
- Morning vs. Afternoon
- Written vs. Spoken word
- Numbers vs. Words.

Do not go through all of these behaviours and try to categorise your colleague on all of the trade-offs. Just think of the four main characteristics of how the person behaves. For example, one manic chief executive I worked with had a very short attention span and very short temper. Monday mornings were the

> he wound himself up like a demented toy soldier

worst: he would have wound himself up like a demented toy soldier over the weekend, and would come in spraying orders and commands everywhere. By Friday afternoon he would have wound down and become calmer and more reflective, especially as most of his colleagues left early on Fridays. So how could I influence him positively? Easy: hang around late on Friday and have a nice informal chat with him when he was calm and not distracted. This was weak on theory, strong in practice. There is no formal psychological analysis tool that would lead you to this insight: a little observation works where a lot of theory fails.

Once you have identified the main behaviours and style of the colleague you want to influence, map them out on a style compass as shown in the example below. For each characteristic you have identified, there is probably an opposite. So in the example below, my colleague is cautious, likes detail, is facts-focused and is best in the morning. The opposite of this would be someone who is risk-taking, big picture- and people-focused.

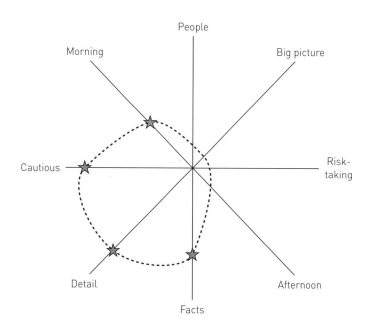

Style compass of my colleague

The style compass gives you a visual map of what this colleague is like. Now you have mapped your colleague, map yourself against the same criteria. Even if other criteria are far more important in shaping your behaviour, ignore them. Your focus is on your colleague's style, not on yourself. You need to see yourself through their eyes, not your eyes. You may overlap completely: in this case you may naturally get on very well together. Or, in this example, you may find that you look very different from your colleague.

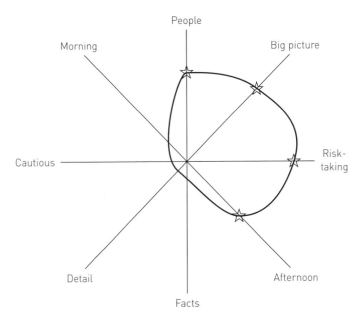

My style compass

Once you have mapped yourself and your colleague, you can take the next obvious step: combine the two style compasses to see how you compare. In this case, my colleague and I are pretty much opposites. This means that we might find it hard to get along, but we could be a very effective combination if we learned to work together. We cancel out each other's weaknesses: I see the big picture, my colleague can fill in the detail. I am a risk junkie, and my colleague might just save me from myself. Equally, I will probably find opportunities which my colleague would avoid. I am good with people and building alliances; my colleague is very good with facts. We could make a very good team, if we knew how to work together. The danger is that we will spend our whole time talking about different things and irritating each other: I will get frustrated by my colleague nagging me for detail and bringing up problems and risks. My colleague will be frustrated that I am all impractical ideas and no recognition of the need to deal with detail, risks and facts. We cannot even agree on the time of day when we should meet.

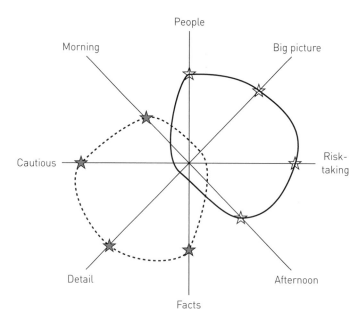

Style compass for my colleague and me

The style compass quickly tells me what I need to do. First, I need to recognise that my colleague may be different, but could be a very valuable ally. I should treasure and cherish this relationship. That means I need to make an effort to adapt to, understand and influence my colleague. To adapt to my colleague I will have to make some adjustments to how I normally work:

- I will make a heroic effort, wake up early and arrange a morning meeting.

- I will make an effort to understand as much detail and as many of the risks of my idea as possible. And I will not roll my eyes in frustration when I am asked for endless amounts of further detail which I probably do not have. I will be prepared for a longer meeting than I like.

- I will ask for help and advice in dealing with the detail and risks and mustering all the facts to make the case: I will recognise him as the expert in these areas and quietly flatter him by deferring to his expertise. I will treat him as an equal partner who plays a vital role in making all this happen.

- I will make my colleague happy by dealing with all the stuff he hates: I will deal with the politics and the people. Where there is risk, I will take the lead in dealing with it.

If I can do all of this, I should avoid an immediate disaster in the form of a massive personality clash. If I do this well, then over time we may well strike up a very productive partnership which plays to our respective strengths.

You can complete the style compass in your head. It is a simple tool to use in advance of any critical meeting. Do it well, and colleagues will find it easy to get along with you: they will not understand or care why they find it easy to work with you. That is the magic of effective influence: it is unseen and apparently unforced. Influence helps people to help you.

Summary

We each live at the centre of our own world. This leads to a very natural and very dangerous mistake. We think that persuading and influencing is about getting our ideas out of our heads and into other people's heads. This leads to a war of the worlds: my world against your world. There is no good outcome to this war. No one surrenders their own world.

Influencers do what Copernicus did 500 years ago. Copernicus rediscovered that the earth is not at the centre of the universe, much to the horror of the Church. Influencers discover that they are not at the centre of the universe. They need to see the world from a different perspective: they need to see the world from the perspective of the people they want to influence. This is the art of walking in other people's shoes.

When we see the world through the eyes of others we do not need to agree with their view or like their view. We only need to understand their view of the world. Their view of the world can normally be summed up in a short

Gossip is good

script about who they are and what they are. It is a self-image which they normally advertise fairly clearly: you do not need to be a genius to work out what people think of themselves. If in doubt, spend some time around the water cooler and listen to the gossip. Gossip is good. In between the nonsense and trivia, there will be nuggets of gold as the characters and actions of colleagues are dissected by the gossips.

Once we understand someone's script and style, we can start to play the right tune the right way. Only when we see our agenda through other people's eyes can we understand what is attractive about it, and what its fatal flaws may be. If we play the right tune, then we will find that we can become the Pied Piper of our firm: everyone will follow us willingly.

Part Four

Seize the moment: make
the most of moments
of truth

Chapter 10

Pick your battles

There are moments when power visibly ebbs and flows between colleagues. At a meeting, one person rises to the challenge where others keep quiet. Two people fall out: one or both of them come out of it worse for wear. A crisis happens and one person deals with it while another fails. An attempt to close the sale succeeds or fails. The moment goes fast, but in that time months of effort are justified or lost, carefully nurtured reputations are built or destroyed.

These moments of truth are rarely random acts of capricious gods. Many of them can be anticipated. Even the unexpected events can be planned for. To build influence, managers have to seize these moments of truth and turn them to their advantage. In any career, there are six highly predictable moments of truth:

1 Negotiating budgets: the art of budget smartball
2 Turning crises into opportunities
3 Dealing with cold wars
4 Surviving hot wars: pick the right battles
5 Finding the right assignment
6 Starting a new role: making a fast start.

Each of these moments of truth will be unique in the way it unfolds. But there are some consistent principles in each case which lead to triumph or disaster. This chapter looks at those principles for each moment of truth.

Negotiating budgets: the art of budget smartball

Budgets are essentially a contract between two levels of management. Top management want to give minimum budget for maximum return. They will dress this up in normal corporate speak. They will talk about 'challenging' budgets and 'stretch' goals. The implication is that you are a wimp if you duck the challenge and you cannot stretch. To make opposition even harder, the budget process tends to be driven top down and from the centre. By the time you are invited to discuss your challenging budget and stretch goals, the decisions have already been taken.

Managers are encouraged to show their machismo by signing up for the targets which will allow the CEO to collect another big bonus and buy a bigger yacht to make other CEOs envy him. This is a good deal for the CEO, less good for you. If you sign up for the macho target you commit yourself to a year of hell. With overwork and stress you may get near your target. For such heroic effort you will get minimal bonus because you did not actually beat your target.

There is an alternative to the budget blues, which a colleague of mine perfected. His name is Paul, and he is one of the idlest leaders I have ever met. He is also very successful and popular, which is deeply irritating. He puts idleness to good advantage. Being idle, he has perfected the art of delegating. Staff love him for it: it shows that he trusts them, and they respond enthusiastically. But there is one period of the year when even he goes into overdrive: budget time.

He starts negotiating the budget long before the budget process formally starts. He carefully sets the scene by reviewing the prospects of his part of the business. This is a short operational and strategic review which senior managers appreciate: it shows that he is on top of his work, is proactive and is helping top managers decide the way forward. Invariably, his review indicates that however good this year has been, next year is likely to be tough in the extreme. He lays out all the initiatives he wants to take (many of which may require investment) and shows that even with all this work, it will be tough to match this year's performance.

By doing this, Paul follows one of the golden rules of winning any battle or discussion: strike early. The purpose of striking early is to anchor the discussion around your agenda. If he let the planning group or CEO anchor the discussion, they would put in a planning assumption based on rapid growth of revenues, no cost increase and dramatic profit improvement. That would commit Paul to a year of hell.

Having made his point, Paul makes it again. And again. And again. And again. And again. He uses every platform and every opportunity to repeat and embellish his position. This is hard work, but hard work for one month negotiating an easy budget is better than 11 months' hard work delivering a tough budget. In the way the corporate world works, if no one challenges a position, it becomes the received wisdom. He turns the tables on the planners: they are used to setting out their position and leaving it to line managers to prove them wrong. He sets out his position and the planners find themselves in the awkward position of having to prove the emerging consensus wrong.

> hard work for one month negotiating an easy budget is better than 11 months' hard work delivering a tough budget

Paul then deploys a third weapon. He begs or borrows as much credibility and authority for his position as possible. He will get marketing and sales to sign off on his market forecasts; he will make sure Finance validates the accuracy of his numbers. He will not ask them to approve his assumptions: that would be an invitation to argue.

Executives often talk about 'playing hardball' on the numbers. Playing hardball is a dumb game. It is about arguing, being obstinate, digging your heels in and losing friends and allies. Paul plays a different game: the winning game is smartball, not hardball. The three golden rules of smartball are:

- Strike early: anchor the discussion on your terms
- Repeat, repeat, repeat: build consensus and momentum
- Build credibility: validate numbers, build buy-in.

Playing budget smartball allows Paul to win without fighting. By the time the formal budget negotiations start he can even afford to be magnanimous and appear macho: he can agree to having his budget stretched because he has already anchored the discussion so far in his favour. This means he sets himself up for 11 months of easy work beating what is perceived to be a stretching target. He gets to be the hero, and we get to be very frustrated.

Turning crisis into opportunity

Crises happen. Staff make mistakes, suppliers let us down, customers change their minds, competitors surprise us. Occasionally, we can even make mistakes ourselves. Crises make and break reputations of companies and individuals. Being the person who takes control and resolves the crisis is the stuff that corporate heroes are made of. Taking the lead feels risky. Leading accelerates your career: you succeed fast or fail fast. Failing to take the lead assures mediocrity.

> Leading accelerates your career: you succeed fast or fail fast

There are two natural and poor reactions to crises. First, deny that there is a problem. When denial becomes impossible, find a scapegoat. The messenger is often a good scapegoat. Denial and blame do not build the reputation of an influential manager.

Denial and blaming make the crisis worse. For instance the British bank HBOS collapsed in 2008 as the result of reckless lending and spiralling bad debt. The cost to the taxpayer exceeds $10 billion.

That is a big crisis. It could have been avoided if the bank had listened to Paul Moore, who was HBOS head of risk and regulatory affairs from 2002 to 2005. He warned the bank of the risks they were running. First they denied it, and then they fired him. Meanwhile, the CEO went on to collect a knighthood for services to banking. Simply, no one wanted to believe there could be a problem, as long as the profits, bonuses and knighthoods were rolling in.

Contrast the HBOS experience with better-managed corporate crises at Tylenol and Perrier:

● *Tylenol*: cyanide was found in some Tylenol capsules in store. Johnson & Johnson did not wait to find out how widespread the problem was or who was to blame. The company recalled all the product nationwide, at a cost of $100 million. That was a small price for protecting and enhancing the firm's reputation. It later turned out that a murderer or ransom artist was responsible.

● *Perrier*: In 1990 some FDA officials found traces of benzene in some Perrier bottles. The FDA spokesman was reassuring about it: 'The hazard would be that over many years, if you consumed about 16 fluid ounces a day, your lifetime risk of cancer might increase by one in a million, which we consider a negligible risk. You don't have to be concerned if you just had a bottle of Perrier.' Nevertheless, Perrier also recalled all the product, which depended on a reputation for purity. A crisis which could have destroyed Perrier's reputation ended up enhancing it.

These successful responses to crises were based on three principles which managers can use in their day-to-day business:

● *Accept that there is a problem*: The longer denial goes on, the worse the crisis becomes.

- *Focus on the solution*: Look forwards, not backwards. Avoid the blame game.

- *Drive to action fast*: Doing something is always better than doing nothing: it may be a small step; it may be a step in the wrong direction. But it shows leadership, creates hope in place of fear and sets the right expectations: action, not analysis will save the day.

Speed is essential. The faster the crisis is resolved, the less time it has to grow out of control. Insurance companies have finally learned this lesson. Progressive Insurance now empowers its loss adjusters to settle claims on the spot, even by the roadside of an accident. This is not just about giving good service. By settling fast the average cost of a claim is reduced by over 20 per cent and the number of complaints reduces by more than 30 per cent.

Inevitably, there are times when everything seems out of control. Lack of control leads first to stress and then to panic. Even in the worst of times, there is always something you can do. It often does not matter how small the action is, or even whether it is the right course of action. The key is to move forwards. For instance, when I was sent to Japan I found the business was dead in the water. It was a hopeless situation: no sales, no clients, no prospects. Morale was sinking like the proverbial lead balloon. In such a hopeless situation we did the only thing we could do: we sold and did more or less any work for any clients. That meant we found ourselves selling Norwegian cheese in Tokyo. We also landed up working alongside Japanese gangsters (the yakuza) on a tobacco project. From such a shaky start we slowly rebuilt sales and morale. They were absolutely the wrong sorts of clients for our business in the long term. But any client was better than none: act fast, drive to action and don't worry about blaming someone for the previous lack of clients.

Conflict management: cold wars

Organisations are set up for conflict. Different departments, functions, business units will have different priorities and perspectives. Internal

> Organisations are set up for conflict

rivalry is a simple way in which to determine the priorities of the organisation as a whole.

If managers want to achieve influence, power or positive outcomes, they cannot avoid conflict. They should embrace it and use it to their advantage. There are occasions where we will need to push our agenda hard, at the risk of inviting conflict. But there will also be many more times when conflict comes knocking on our door, uninvited. To maintain influence we need to deal with such conflict well.

Cold wars are the slow, festering disputes over projects, people, priorities and principles. They can go on for an eternity, which in corporate terms means until the next reorganisation happens. First, managers have to decide if the cold war is worth fighting.

Some 2500 years ago, the Chinese philosopher Sun Tzu wrote *The Art of War*. Even then, he recognised that war is not always the best way of achieving your goals. He laid out three conditions which had to be satisfied before it was worth going to war:

- Only fight when there is a prize worth fighting for
- Only fight when you know you will win
- Only fight when there is no other way of achieving your goals.

As you look at the many corporate battles that fester inside your own organisation, you will probably find that many of them fail at least one of Sun Tzu's tests. Some of them will fail all three tests: many corporate battles amount to little more than the ritual rutting of stags trying to claim dominance over each other. Such battles are highly emotionally charged. Logic, facts, reason are merely used as fuel for the emotional fire. While such battles may be amusing to watch, they are damaging to conduct. Even if you win the argument, you lose a friend. There will be plenty of opportunity for them to take revenge later: they can quietly poison the well of public opinion against you; they can undermine your initiatives with passive and covert resistance; they may even be promoted ahead of you. Sun Tzu recognised a basic reality of corporate life: it is better to have an army of allies than an army of enemies.

> it is better to have an army of allies than an army of enemies

Each war unfolds in its own messy way. The fog of war makes it hard to know what is going on or what the next step is to be. There are always fine judgement calls to be made about what to do, who to talk to and in what order events should happen. In such uncertainty it helps to have some guiding principles. Start with Sun Tzu to decide if you should be fighting at all. If you must, then there are two further principles to rely on:

- Build a coalition of support
- Fight on your terms, not theirs.

The need for a coalition has been dealt with extensively in 'Weave your web' (Part Three). You need quality, not just quantity of support. Once you have mustered enough of an army, the opposition will often melt away: they have no need to go into a glorious and gory defeat.

The second factor is the David and Goliath principle. Even if you appear to face strong opposition, you can succeed by changing the terms of debate. This is a lesson that insurgents and terrorists learn early. You cannot beat highly equipped and trained forces on their own terms. Instead, they indulge in asymmetric warfare: they fight in a way that nullifies the technical and manpower advantages of conventional forces.

Much successful corporate strategy is based on the idea of asymmetric warfare. If you want to take on a Goliath, compete on different terms. Ryanair has become larger than BA in terms of passengers, flights and market value from nowhere in 15 years. It succeeded not by taking on BA on its own terms, but having a different business model which can be summed up on one word: cheap. This gets dressed up in fancy ways as 'Blue Ocean' thinking, complete with value curves, strategic intent and core competences. You do not need fancy language to work out 'cheap'. The idea of asymmetric warfare applies within firms as well.

For instance, one employer had a long-running war over how fast to expand its graduate recruiting programme. Half the management team were bullish and wanted rapid growth, the other half was bearish and wanted to consolidate. Both sides amassed huge amounts of data which proved their point. It was like trench warfare: it was a bloody stalemate. The CEO was caught between both sides. So he changed the terms of the debate. He claimed he did not care about the numbers (he did care, but did not want to take sides). He set a challenge instead: recruit as many as you want provided they hit the new quality bar I am setting. By changing the debate from quantity to quality the war ended and peace broke out.

There is an alternative to the Sun Tsu doctrine: the Nelson doctrine. Admiral Nelson gave his captains a simple order: 'any captain who lays his ship alongside that of the enemy (to fight them) can do no wrong'. This was the ultimate power play. He would have captains going halfway round the world to find the enemy and pick a fight. Some fights appeared insane. Lord Cochrane made his name as the captain of a small frigate by taking on and beating a Spanish warship: it was like a minesweeper defeating an aircraft carrier today. The effect of the Nelson doctrine was dramatic. The enemy did not dare leave port because they knew the fate that awaited them. And the more the navy fought, the better they got at it. Some executives follow the same strategy. They can become very powerful bullies. But eventually they pick the wrong fight and acquire too many enemies. Nelson lost an eye, an arm and then his life. Nelson had influence which lasted well beyond his death. But for most executives, career death is not the path to lasting influence.

Conflict management: hot wars, from FEAR to EAR

Some cold wars turn hot very fast. A crisis, cock-up or misunderstanding happens. Suddenly, tempers flare. Emails and phones start to glow red hot with indignation, anger, denial, blame. Reason is buried by emotion. In conflict, managers use facts like drunks use lamp posts: for support, not illumination. The first step with a hot war is to recognise that

> managers use facts like drunks use lamp posts: for support, not illumination

underneath they are mainly about emotion and politics. At this point there are two ways of reacting: the FEAR or EAR response.

The FEAR response is common. It stands for:

Fight furiously

Engage enemy emotionally

Argue against anyone

Retaliate, repudiate reason.

This is not a productive way to fight a conflict, although it can be fun. Especially if it is your last day at the firm.

If we want to respond more productively, we need to remove the F (for fear) from FEAR: we are then left with EAR. EAR sums up what we should focus on: listening. The more we listen and understand, the better we can respond. EAR stands for:

Empathise

Agree the problem

Resolve the way forward.

The angrier someone is, the more important empathy becomes. Let them blow off steam. Try screaming in anger for more than one minute: it is very hard to sustain emotion for long. It takes too much effort, unless we receive some emotional fuel for our anger from someone else. Deny them the fuel. This needs a little sensitivity. If you say something like 'I understand how you feel' you simply invite another explosion which starts 'No, you don't understand how I feel!'

Once someone has calmed down, it is time to find out what really happened. Do not try to defend or justify your position: that simply leads to an argument again. The goal is to reach understanding about what the problem is and what they want. Start to focus on the desired outcome. Use listening skills: ask open questions and paraphrase what they say to demonstrate that you have heard and understood their position.

Resolving the way forward is often the easiest part of the process: if they have calmed down, explained the situation and identified the desired outcome, they should be ready to agree how to get there. At this stage, avoid getting stuck in a single-point solution if possible: 'do this by this time' is a win-lose ultimatum. You are now essentially in a negotiation about what to do. Follow basic negotiation principles: create a win-win situation; generate more than one solution; discuss alternatives; know your bottom line.

It can be difficult to remain calm while a fat, pompous, bullying boss or client is jabbing their finger at you at making all sorts of inflammatory remarks. I asked Sue, who maintains a more or less Zen-like detachment in even the most dire situations, how she remains so calm, poised and professional. It is a style which makes her hugely admired. 'Easy,' she said. 'I just imagine the other person dressed in a pink tutu. It is very hard to get angry with a fat 50-year-old making a fool of themself in a tutu. My problem is not getting angry. My problem is to avoid laughing.'

Sue's secret does not work for everyone. So I asked other clients how they dealt with such moments. They all had little mind tricks they used. Here are a few alternatives:

- Imagine someone you deeply admire: what would they do in this situation? We all have role models we aspire to: copy them. If you most admire Darth Vader or Vlad the Impaler, do not use this trick – although one executive wipes out his opposition with an imaginary Uzi. It makes him feel much better after seeing their blood splattered all over the wall.

- Become a fly on the wall: look down on the situation and decide on the best thing to do.

- Go silent. Let the other person burn out. Give yourself time to think. Count to 10 (just like your granny told you to), breathe deeply, retain your composure and gather your thoughts. Silence can be very unnerving for both sides.

● Focus on the outcome you want in 15 minutes' time: reach beyond the immediate crisis. This will eventually set the discussion in the right direction and will make you appear positive and professional.

Assignments and projects

In every firm there are dream projects and death star projects. Finding the right role, assignment or project is vital. Cleaning toilets in Siberia may be presented to you as an exotic, important and worthy challenge, but it will not be a great way to build power and influence. Being tapped on the shoulder to work in the CEO's office for a year will probably move you further ahead. It pays to find the right opportunity.

Normally, the decision is not as clear-cut as between the CEO's office and Siberian toilets. Many coaching sessions have focused on this problem. Solving the problem turns on answering four questions:

1 Will I enjoy the assignment?

2 Am I set up for success?

3 Will I build skills and reputation?

4 What is the alternative?

As ever, the questions are easier than the answers.

Will I enjoy the assignment?

The enjoyment question surprises people. Business is meant to be Serious. Serious people are not meant to have fun. But enjoyment is fundamental to success. You only excel at what you enjoy. It is impossible to

> You only excel at what you enjoy

find any star of film or sports who dislikes what they do. Even those business people who complain loudly about all the travel, work and long hours they have to do are not complaining: they are boasting about how important they are. And if we are going to have to commit a large part of our waking hours to an assignment, we need stamina to sustain ourselves. It is hard to sustain commitment to something we do not like. So if the heart sinks at the prospect of a new assignment, role, project or boss, listen to the heart. Find something which lifts your spirits rather than sinks them.

Many opportunities are presented as challenges. In business speak 'challenge' is a euphemism for a disaster. That is not necessarily a bad opportunity. If you want to prove yourself then, in which of these two set-ups will you make a positive difference?

- Role A: you inherit a business which is performing at its peak: it already has market leadership, exceptional profitability and is run as a very lean machine.
- Role B: you inherit a basket case: inefficient, losing money and market share and lousy morale in the team.

It is very hard to improve anything in Role A, although you will get plenty of visibility with top management. Even modest changes should have a dramatic difference in Role B, where you have the chance to be a hero. You could also sink with the ship in Role B.

Am I set up for success?

To understand if you are set up for success, ask a few more questions:

- How good is the team?
- What is the boss like?
- What level of political sponsorship and support is there for this role?
- Is there enough budget and resource to succeed?
- Are the expectations of success realistic?

You will probably get ambiguous answers and mixed signals in reply to these questions. Things are rarely clear and simple in business. Do not accept ambiguity. The fog of uncertainty is usually a smokescreen to hide some unpleasant surprises. If you get unclear answers, press hard. First, get clarity if you can. If you still do not like the answers, negotiate hard. Make sure that you set yourself up for success by getting the right resources, goals and support. As soon as you accept the role, your ability to negotiate vanishes. Before you accept, you have the chance to set expectations and negotiate the right terms. Use that window of opportunity well.

Will I build the right skills and reputation?

This question looks to the longer term. Building a career and influence is a marathon, not a sprint. It requires building the right skills and capabilities. Put simply, the rules of success and survival change at every level of the firm. Junior staff learn technical skills: bookkeeping, trading, PowerPoint or law. Top managers are rarely called on to do the stock-check. They need a different skill set: strategy; managing politics, teams and stakeholders; financial insight and discipline. It pays to acquire the skills which will set you up for the next stage of the journey.

Many people get caught by the skills trap. They develop a technical expertise which is highly valued, but is useless in helping them progress. For instance, one of the brightest associates I worked with became a world expert in modelling the tripartite asset collateralised repo market. The what market? It was so obscure I did not even know it existed. But, as with many financial markets, it is so large it is hard to count the number of zeros at the end of each transaction. Because he was so good at the modelling, he kept on being asked to do more of the same. It was valuable work for the firm and a dead end for him: he could not possibly build a career out of his work, and he was not learning the skills needed to become a manager.

We can learn technical skills like accounting from training courses. But the skills we really need, about leading other people and making things happen, we learn from a combination of personal experience and role models. That is why getting the right assignment is essential. The right assignment not only gives you the chance to develop useful skills, but it also exposes you to successful role models who you can watch and learn from.

What is the alternative?

The fourth and final question is a killer: what is the alternative? You may not like the idea of cleaning toilets in Siberia, but if the alternative is working in the salt mine, you may well want to volunteer quickly for the Siberian toilets. This is not a pleasant choice. The solution is clear: make sure you have some good alternatives.

Keeping some options open is a basic of career management. Becoming dependent on one boss, one role, one skill set is a recipe for slavery and ultimately for career suicide. Such people turn out to be very dispensable in a crunch, and they have nowhere else to go. To keep options open, everyone needs a good radar to pick up on emerging opportunities early; to identify who is hot and who is not; who to work with and who to avoid. Where there are good opportunities, be helpful and enthusiastic. Where there are unpleasant opportunities emerging, assume Harry Potter's cloak of invisibility: make yourself very busy and indispensable in your existing work.

> Becoming dependent on one boss is a recipe for slavery

Making a fast start

Moving into a new role is a wonderful opportunity for personal reinvention. I discovered this when I went to Japan. No one there knew me. They had no idea what my strengths or weaknesses might be. I was a blank canvas. I could draw myself however I wanted to be. It was liberating to leave behind the baggage of perceptions from the home office, both positive and negative. Even smaller moves within a firm offer the chance for reinvention: you can play up strengths, minimise weaknesses and try some new skills and tricks. But very quickly, opinions and prejudices will be formed. Once opinion has been anchored around a certain image, it is very difficult to shift opinion. Making a fast start and anchoring the right expectations is essential.

There are four elements to making a fast start successful:

- Write your own script
- Set the right expectations
- Tell a story
- Pick the right team.

Write your own script

Writing your own script is about knowing what you want to do and how you want to be in your new role. Give yourself clear expectations about what good looks like. And then think about how you want to be: how you will be different from the past, what skills you will develop, the style you will manage. All of this needs to be done before you take up the new role. After a month, judgement will have been passed: your team and bosses will have decided what you are like and where you are going. For instance, Andrew was intellectually clever, but was impatient with people. Before going into a new role, he made one simple decision: he would make a conscious effort to listen longer to team members. He did not try to transform himself into a touchy-feely tree-hugger, because he knew he could not do that: it would not be authentic. But he could manage to listen more. That one small act transformed perceptions of him in his new role: he was suddenly seen as a sympathetic and effective leader who was good with people.

Set the right expectations

Setting the right expectations also has to be done before you start a new role. The chances are the person you are replacing has painted a picture of a job well done with everything poised for stunning success. This is a poisoned chalice. If that is the accepted version of events, you cannot win. If you do well, it will be because of the great groundwork of your predecessor. If things go wrong, it will be because you screwed up. Reset expectations fast. Show that, despite appearances, everything is on the brink of total collapse. If this version of the truth is accepted, then averting disaster will make you into a hero. The same modest performance can be seen as success or failure, depending on how you set expectations. This is not devious practice by a few middle managers: this is standard practice. Take time to see how many new CEOs suddenly discover the need for huge write-offs and write-downs caused by their foolish predecessors: they are simply setting shareholder expectations and creating a low base from which they can easily improve performance.

Tell a story

> For every great visionary who leads you to the promised land, there are a dozen more who lead you straight back into the desert

Telling a story is about having a vision and a strategy. Every firm and department needs a vision about where they are going. Having a vision and a strategy is different from being a visionary. For every great visionary who leads you to the promised land, there are a dozen more who lead you straight back into the desert. A vision and a strategy has to be much more practical. A good vision is no more than a story in three parts:

1   This is where we are

2   This is where we are going

3   This is how we will get there.

Looked at this way, anyone can create a vision for their part of the business. Having the story is vital to perceptions and influence. Many colleagues and bosses will only have a vague idea of what you really do. Even non-executive directors can be very unclear about things like the strategy of their firm. But if you give them a story to tell, they can trot off to the opera or the golf happily retelling the story to their friends. The 'how we will get there' statement needs to be kept simple if it is to be remembered. It can come down to a campaign theme for the year ahead such as:

- Cutting costs
- Being more professional
- Increasing customer focus.

A good, simple story gives everyone direction and focus. It helps people remember what you stand for and gives the impression that you have a plan and are making a difference. These are good impressions for an influencer to create.

Pick the right team

Picking the right team is vital. A good team walks on water. A weak team drowns and will bring you down with it. This is another BFO: Blinding Flash of the Obvious. It is only worth restating because it is routinely ignored. Many managers assume that the team they inherit is the team they must work with. This dangerous assumptions leads to tears; you may get lucky with the team you inherit but you may not. If you choose to rely on luck, you may as well rely on fortune tellers and tarot cards.

The art of team formation relies heavily on trading and dealing with colleagues. Giving team members options elsewhere in the organisation is smoother and easier than trying to fire everyone. The influencer who has weaved a strong web of influence can find reasonable alternatives for team members who need to be shifted. Equally, it makes sense to invest in romancing people you want to attract into your team. All of this is seriously hard work. It requires give and take: everyone wants to offload their weak players and avoid taking on the unknown, new or weak staff. Like NFL player trades, the goal is not to get the 20 best players: they may all be quarterbacks. The goal is to get a balanced team: it is in the search for balance that trade becomes possible. If you have two good quarterbacks, one can be traded for a couple of other positions where you have weaknesses.

Summary: style and substance

In all moments of truth you will be judged not just by what you do, but how you do it. Bystanders, including bosses, find it very difficult to know who was responsible for what and who was to blame. The facts of each case tend to be murky and contradictory. The 'I said he said she said I said' conversation only makes things worse. Bosses do not want to hear who said or did what. They will not understand the history and probably will not care for it much either. They want to know how to move forward.

Even if history is foggy, the present is very clear. Moments of truth are life lived with the record button on and in full Technicolor: everyone remembers such moments well. That is why they make or break reputations. Long after the detail of exactly what happened has been forgotten, how people conducted themselves will be remembered. That means that style is as important as substance. The good news is that unprofessional behaviour helps the influential manager. The more unprofessionally everyone else behaves, the easier it is for the influential manager to establish a positive reputation.

Look at some of your positive and negative role models: how have they conducted themselves at moments of truth? You can create your own checklist of dos and don'ts. Some of the more common dos and don'ts people identify are shown below:

Don'ts	Dos
Hide	Step up
Be negative	Be positive
Look back, analyse	Look forward, find solutions
Be angry	Be calm
Blame, divide	Support, cooperate
Focus on problems	Drive to action

As with much of influence this is obvious. There are no dark secrets here, just common sense. But many managers leave common sense behind in the car park. If you can bring your

> many managers leave common sense behind in the car park

common sense into the office, and apply it consistently, you can stand out positively and build your influence.

Chapter 11
Win-win

enry Kissinger was Secretary of State for the United States during the Vietnam War. He was used to high-level politics and diplomacy. But he found that far easier than university politics. Dealing with professors was harder than dealing with presidents: 'university politics are so vicious precisely because the stakes are so small,' he said. As Secretary of State he had large stakes: he could offer trade deals and aid deals; intelligence support and military support; he also had plenty of sanctions to threaten or use. In a university, only one person can sit in the professor's chair. Small stakes, big politics. The same problem affects every firm. The stakes are too small. Being creative with stakes is essential to influence.

Managers compete heavily for the same limited pot of management time, budget, bonus and promotion. The real competition is not in the marketplace: it is sitting at a desk near you. The result is a macho world of win–lose. As ever, however, the best way to win is without fighting. This is the subtle art of the win–win. If you use influence well, most battles can be avoided. The art is to win while letting the other side think that they have won as well. The art of the win–win is a basic principle of negotiation, both within the firm and with third parties.

> The real competition is not in the marketplace: it is sitting at a desk near you.

The five main strands of achieving a win–win discussion are:

- Focus on interests, not positions
- Offer options
- Make a symbolic concession
- Craft a story
- Public private partnership.

These five themes can be found in the unlikely world of selling labels for soup tins. Selling labels for soup tins is not glamorous, but it is necessary. Inevitably, the buyer wanted a lower price. He always wanted a lower price. That is all he could think about because that is how he showed he was doing a good job. The salesman had to maximise his selling price. Every meeting became an argument. Both sides had a very clear position which could be expressed as a price.

One day, the salesman did something odd. He asked if he could tour the soup plant: he wanted to see what happened to his labels. Relieved to have a discussion that was not an argument, the buyer agreed. They toured the factory and talked to various managers about what they wanted from the soup labels. The scheduler was frustrated: it was very difficult to predict demand. He often needed quick turnaround on the supply of labels: if there was a cold snap, then soup sales would soar and they would run out of soup labels. Labels represented 0.1 per cent of the cost of the soup, but without the label, they would lose 100 per cent of the sales.

The marketing manager was also frustrated. He often needed short runs for promotions or for test markets. Like the scheduler, the cost of the labels was more or less irrelevant. He needed flexible design and fast turnaround. The production manager, meanwhile, cursed the marketing manager. To be efficient, he wanted nice long runs of tomato soup. All the changing over between flavours and designs was a pain in the backside which interrupted the efficient flow of production.

The vendor and the buyer returned to the office, thinking. Perhaps the label maker could do more to help the soup maker: short runs, quick turnaround and flexible design seemed to be at least as important as price. Suddenly the vendor and buyer had more to talk about. The label maker could help the soup maker sell more and make more money by offering short runs and quick turnarounds. And the soup maker would pay more for this. This allowed the salesman to offer a further reduction on the price of labels for long runs of tomato soup: he was making up for that price concession with price gains elsewhere. In return he got guarantees of long runs and high volumes. The label maker won (higher prices on special runs) and the buyer won (help the soup company make more money).

The soup story illustrates the main points of a successful win–win:

- *Interests not positions*: the price argument was win–lose. Helping the soup manufacturer make money was a win–win.
- *Deal in private, not public*: The negotiations took place in the buyer's office. If they had taken place elsewhere in the factory, the buyer would have found it difficult to be so flexible.

- *Offer more than one choice*: move the discussion away from price and on to other things which might be of value to the soup maker

- *Craft a story*: the salesman was giving the buyer a chance to show he was not just tough (on price) but he was also smart (improving firm profitability). The win was not just a rational win for the company: it was a personal win for the buyer.

- *Give and take.* By creating options, the buyer was able to offer concessions on price (for tomato soup labels) and gain a return on both volumes (tomato soup) and on price (special runs).

Below, we will explore how to apply these five principles of influencing in practice.

Focus on interests, not positions

Sarah taught in a challenging inner-city school. She had done extremely well in her first two years at the school. She felt she was now due a pay rise and a promotion. The head teacher had little budget and not much flexibility on grades and promotions. Sarah and the head teacher had completely opposite positions: pay rise and promotion versus no rise and no promotion. War loomed. How could they avoid a win–lose battle over their respective positions?

Fortunately, they both had a passionate commitment to improving the life chances of inner-city kids. They had a common interest at a very high level, but there was still a huge gap to convert that interest into a practical way forward. Being a teacher, Sarah did her homework before meeting the head teacher. She figured out they had three further common interests:

- She wanted to stay; the head needed her to stay. Attracting quality staff was time-consuming, expensive and fraught with risk.

- She wanted more responsibility; the head had several programmes around behaviour management and a literacy drive which needed a team leader.

- She wanted to build her career and get a Master's degree: the head was under pressure to show the school governors what he was doing about professional development.

When they met, the head was mightily relieved to find that Sarah did not ask for the expected pay rise and promotion. It was a much more useful discussion about what she would do if she stayed. Eventually, they agreed that she would lead the literacy drive across the school, which would give her credits towards the Master's degree she was working on.

Finally, Sarah asked the head how he could help on pay and position. Too late, the head realised he had been put on the spot. He had to do something for Sarah. There was a long pause. He realised that with Sarah leading the literacy drive, that would save costs versus bringing in outside help. Retaining Sarah would also save on the costs and risks of recruiting a replacement. Sarah was helping him save some precious budget: he could afford to share some of the savings with her. In the end Sarah got less than she had asked for, but more than she had expected. More important, both Sarah and the head left feeling that they had achieved a very satisfactory outcome. Neither had achieved their original positions, but they had fulfilled their common interests.

Win–lose discussions are natural, but unproductive. If you win an argument, you lose an ally. Influencers learn winning allies is more important than winning arguments in the long term. When it comes to the next discussion, the loser in a win–lose discussion will be out for revenge. In contrast, the influencers have much easier rides to a win-win with their allies. Focusing on common interests rather than individual positions is the first step towards achieving a win–win.

> If you win an argument, you lose an ally

Offer options

I went to a store to buy a computer. The store manager and I did not have much of a common interest. The manager wanted to make as much money, and I wanted to spend as little money as possible for my new computer. I figured I had $1000 to spend. It looked like we were going to have a head-on collision over price.

But the store manager was smart. First, he took time to listen to what I wanted: good start. Then he suggested a computer which was below my budget: very smart. This showed I could trust him. He was not trying to escalate me into a higher price bracket. And then he confused me, which was really smart. He bamboozled me with choice.

First of all, there is a choice of computers and trade-offs around countless features: memory, speed, storage, graphics and much more. Even with a settled configuration, there is more choice: what software will be bundled; service and warranty guarantees; delivery and set-up; financing (outright purchase versus leasing). The choice is bewildering. I now realised that focus on price was too simple: I needed to think harder about lifetime cost and value.

By the time I had worked through all the choices, my head was reeling. Fortunately, the sales manager made it easy for me. He reduced the choice back down to just two packages which seemed to suit me best: one at $25 a month for three years, the other at $35 a month. To make it easy for me, he threw in some extra software, an extra year of warranty and a data transfer package into the deal on the higher price package. He had offered me a concession, an apparent win. It was a concession which was standard practice, but it gave me the sense I was winning. I bought and was happy to have got a bargain … which had cost me more than I had originally budgeted.

By offering choice, the manager got away from the simple price discussion. It was now a price–value discussion. A price discussion is win–lose. Price–value can be a win–win discussion.

Many head-on clashes can be avoided by changing the terms of
the debate and offering options and alternatives. These alternatives
will normally get away from haggling over positions to a richer
discussion around interests, as outlined in the previous section.
Typical examples of changing the terms of the debate include:

- From price to value
- From quantity to quality
- From inputs to outputs (the cost of soup labels to the profits
  of making soup)
- From job promotion to personal development.

Make a symbolic concession

Negotiators like to think they have won. Let them think that. Have
some concessions ready which will let them brag, let them build a
story to convince themselves and others that they have won. The
concessions can be symbolic as much as substantive. For instance,
in selling professional services clients always wince when
presented with the cost. They are right to wince: the bills are
painful. But they find it hard to negotiate on price, because it is
hard for them to size and price the job accurately. But they want to
know that they are getting a good deal. So we offer them other
things to negotiate about, which we will let them win:

- *Start date*: even if we are flexible, we let clients negotiate for
  and 'win' their preferred start date.
- *Team leader*: clients will hook onto one or two people they have
  seen in the sales process: even if they are already available, we
  will play hard to get and then 'concede': we will assign the
  person they want to the team.
- *Quality assurance*: we will let clients build break points into the
  programme where they can decide to go on or cut off. In
  practice, once started the programmes are nearly impossible to
  stop, but it is a comforting concession for them.

These concessions are more about perceptions than reality. Managers often find it hard to negotiate the really big issues: they are too big and too complex. They are like the drunk that loses his keys in a dark alley at night: he then looks for the keys in the street because that is where the light is and he can see more clearly. Managers negotiate what is easy, not what is important.

> Managers negotiate what is easy, not what is important

This became clear at a very tense board meeting after a merger: the board spent an hour discussing whether to let the staff have a glass of champagne to celebrate the merger. One side said alcohol in working hours set a bad example. The other side said management needed to show their appreciation. And because there were no vested interests at stake, everyone could pontificate about principles at great length. As time was running out before lunch, the chairman wanted to draw the meeting to a close. The IT director pounced: 'Before we close, can we just approve my paper on IT integration strategy?' Marketing, HR, Finance and Counsel all looked blank: IT integration was an alien concept to them. They nodded their approval. With that, 1000 jobs went, one IT supplier lost $100 million which went to a rival and a small town suffered a huge leap in unemployment. Managers prefer to discuss what is easy, not what is important.

Craft a story

No one likes to lose. And who thinks they are below average when it comes to living, loving, driving or shopping? Effective influencers understand how to use these perceptions well. The goal is to let people convince themselves that they have succeeded. They need to tell their friends, colleagues and bosses that they have been smart and achieved a good outcome. Successful negotiations are as much about perceptions as about reality: it is about emotion as much as about reason.

> Successful negotiations are as much about perceptions as about reality

Success needs to be wrapped up in an easy statement or story that can be retold to anyone who will listen. Review the stories in this chapter. Each time the influencer left the target with a story which would make them look good, despite moving away from their original position.

● The soup label buyer: helped the firm make more money by supporting demand surges and special promotions better (but paid more for the labels)

● The head teacher: retained a star teacher, solved the problem of the literacy drive, avoided expensive recruitment costs and showed the governors a good example of professional development (but spent a bit more money and gave away some grade inflation)

● The computer buyer: got a great deal on financing, service and set-up together with some free software: good deal (but the overall cost was higher than he had planned).

These stories allow people to look good to themselves and to their peers. The smart influencer will reinforce these stories by congratulating the target on how well they have done; or by explaining that they have conceded more than they had expected. It is simple flattery which burnishes the ego and reinforces the target's confidence and self-image. It costs nothing but builds confidence.

Public private partnerships

As soon as someone says something in public, they are committed. They cannot unwind their position without loss of face. Notice how politicians go through yoga-like contortions to avoid changing a public position, even when any sane view of their situation would demand a change. In the workplace, as soon as someone says 'that won't work…' they are committed: they will then find more or less any reason to justify their initial instinct.

For the purposes of influencing, the critical distinction is between public and private. Any meeting where there are more than two people present is public. Introducing a third person means that the discussion is no longer in confidence.

For this reason, most influencing happens quietly behind closed doors and on a one-to-one basis. The purpose of a meeting, for an influencer, is never to make a decision. The value of a public meeting (with more than two people present) is to give public confirmation to all the deals that have been struck in private. Each person around the table wants the comfort of knowing that they are not alone in supporting your brilliant or crazy idea. Collective agreement is important: if everyone agrees then no one can be singled out if things go wrong later on.

If there is one person who cannot be influenced in private, then at least the private discussions allow you to do three things which help:

- You understand why the person disagrees: you can narrow the disagreement down to one or two highly specific issues

- You build up a coalition of support which isolates the person who disagrees: once they see the power of the coalition they will normally back down, having made their various points

- You have followed fair process: you have given the individual a chance to be heard. This show of respect will draw much of the sting and venom out of the opposition.

Keep doubts and opposition in private; make agreements public.

Summary

Win–win is about mindset and creativity.

The win–win mindset depends on seeing the world through the eyes of the person you wish to influence. You cannot offer them a win unless you know what a win looks like for them. And the good news is that the win for them is as much about perception as about reality. Find a concession, an offer which will make them look good in their own eyes and in the eyes of their peers.

To find the win-win requires creativity. Creativity can come from innate genius on the spur of the moment and some of it can come from experience. A more reliable way of being creative is to work as a team. Prepare sales calls, negotiations and important meetings with the help of your team. The more you discuss it, the more options, potential concessions and win-wins will appear. You will gain more insight into how the other party thinks. Spontaneity is best when it is well rehearsed.

> Spontaneity is best when it is well rehearsed

The win–lose mindset can win today's battle. But it makes it much harder to win tomorrow's battle: the loser will be twice as resistant next time around. The win-win allows you to win without fighting today. It then makes it even easier to win again next time, because you have an ally not an enemy.

Chapter 12

Persuasive
conversations

The dark arts of persuasion cover many sins: bribery, blackmail, bullying, deceit, deception, cold calling and plain persistence can all work. Attractive and effective as many of these tools may seem, we will set them to one side. None of them are needed for a manager to be influential. There is a subtler art of persuasion which all managers must eventually learn if they are to succeed. This is the art of the persuasive conversation: convincing others to support you and your ideas. Do this well and they will follow you willingly, not reluctantly. It is like magic to control such conversations and persuade colleagues to support you.

A persuasive conversation is essentially a sales pitch. Many managers do not like to think of themselves as salespeople. But if they are to be influential, they have to learn the art of persuading and selling. The more senior managers become, the more important selling becomes. CEOs are essentially salespeople: they are pitching their ideas to stakeholders inside and outside the company. One CEO reckoned that over half of his time in a major two-year restructuring was spent talking, listening and persuading. The traditional tasks of deciding strategy, allocating resources and monitoring performance were trivial compared to the sales task. Managers at all levels need to master selling and persuasive conversations if they are to promote and protect their agendas successfully.

All persuasive conversations have the same structure, although the conversation may last from two minutes to two years. It is a structure I learned when selling nappies in Birmingham. I have used it since to start a bank, sell consulting in Japan and persuade colleagues to lend their support. The context, goals, culture and time frame change, but the structure does not. The basic seven-step structure is this:

1 Preparation
2 Alignment
3 Agree the problem or opportunity
4 Explore benefits and outcomes
5 Outline solutions
6 Pre-empt/resolve problems
7 Close.

To show how fast this structure can flow, let's look at a simplified example. The team had been working late and wanted to keep working. I thought they all needed a break if they were to be productive the next day: time to get them out of the office and down to the bar:

1 Preparation: make sure the whole team was in the room. Check with a couple of them that they were as tired as they looked. Ask for their attention.

2 Alignment: 'It's been a hard week, how are you all feeling?' Groans of tiredness and mutterings of discontent were all that came by way of reply.

3 Agree the problem/opportunity: 'We're all tired. We need a break.'

4 Explore benefits and outcomes: 'We need to be fresh for tomorrow, and a bit more team morale would not be bad either.'

5 Outline solution: 'Let's go to the bar around the corner.'

6 Pre-empt and resolve problems: 'I'll buy the first round.'

7 Close: 'Last person out buys the second round.'

That persuasive conversation lasted seconds before the stampede to the door started. Other conversations are not quite so easy, take more time and require more finesse.

To illustrate the structure we will use one main case, and refer to a few others. The main case was an unexpected challenge. We were in Tokyo. A bank called us and said they would like to talk to us about cutting costs. We heard that they had already informally agreed to work with McKinsey, with whom they shared the same building, on the project. We had not worked with them before: we were being brought in mainly to keep McKinsey honest on fees. Our challenge was clear: displace the preferred supplier and win the contract.

As we work through the seven stages of a persuasive conversation, there are seven principles to remember. These principles put into practice many of the principles of influence:

1   The noddy principle: An effective conversation has your opposite number nodding in agreement from the start. You may start simply by agreeing that it is a rainy or sunny day. But start the agreement process early. Do not start with the most contentious issue first: once they start disagreeing, they will continue to do so. The idea is to slowly funnel the discussion towards its desired outcome.

2   Win-win principle: A win–lose discussion is a conflict. Identify how you can both win and you will have a much more productive conversation.

3   The emotional engagement principle: it is easy to disagree with people you dislike, harder to argue against people you like. Get onto your counterpart's wavelength early. If they annoy you, do not show it.

> it is easy to disagree with people you dislike

4 Other people's shoes principle: Do not try to batter people into submission with the brilliance of your idea and logic. See how it looks from their side: what's in it for them, why they might object and what you can do to prevent them objecting.

5 The options principle: Have a best-case option and be prepared to work backwards from it. Anchor the discussion early around your best case: it is easier to concede than it is to have an agreement and then ask for more. Set expectations well from the start. Stay open to new ideas: you may improve on your best option.

6 The partnership principle: You are neither telling someone, nor being told, what to do. You are working together to discover a good outcome. That means you should try to listen twice as much as you talk. You should also look and act the part of a partner, not a salesman.

7 The logic principle: The seven steps are a flow. Do not get ahead of yourself: take your time and make sure each step is complete before moving to the next. The only exception is the close: if someone wants to agree with you, let them agree: do not spend more time talking and persuading. You may say something which unsells your idea.

The conversation structure and principles are the 7x7 sales and persuasion model. Do not try to remember all of it all at once. Try one thing at a time, and progress from there. Everyone has their own unique style and way of deploying the model: it is not a mechanistic script which you have to read. To start with, focus on the first step (preparing the conversation) and try deploying whichever of the seven principles you feel most comfortable with. With practice you can build up more steps and more principles. By way of consolation, rest assured that even the most accomplished salespeople still mess up and are still learning after decades of experience. The goal is not perfection. The goal is improvement.

Preparation

Social conversations can be an enjoyable random walk of discovery. Business does not succeed on the basis of a random walk. To make progress, there has to be a purpose to a conversation. That requires preparation. The preparation may take 15 seconds as you walk towards someone's office, or it may take days as you prepare for a big meeting. The checklist covers the following five questions:

1 What do I want to achieve in this meeting?
   ● What is my Plan B which takes me halfway to the goal?
2 How will the other person see this issue?
   ● what are their no-go areas?
   ● What are their hot buttons: what will turn them on?
   ● Why would they want to support this idea?
3 How should I interact with them? What is their style?
4 Are any logistics required for the meeting: phones, conference numbers, flip charts, room layout, number of people, room bookings, etc.
5 How will I start the meeting?

For our first formal meeting with the Tokyo bank we spent several days doing our homework: finding out as much about the business as possible, who was going to be at the meeting and what, if anything, we knew about them. Having found out that the competition was McKinsey, we realised there was no point in going head to head with a smarty-pants presentation. We would have to change the rules of the game and have a more interactive and more participative meeting. We set this expectation, making it clear that it would be an example of the way we would run the project with them.

We also sent in advance a short summary of our relevant credentials: we did not want to waste time in the meeting boasting about ourselves. We wanted to engage the client and make them start talking instead of hearing us pitch and judging us. Although we were going to have a discussion, not a presentation, the preparation was intense. We had to prepare for all the different ways in which the discussion could go, and we very tightly scripted the outcome we actually wanted. Preparing a presentation takes less time because there is less interaction and fewer variables to worry about.

Alignment

This is where you need to start walking in the other person's shoes. You need to help them answer some questions which they will have in their heads:

- What is this discussion all about?
- Why should I talk to this person about this subject?
- Why am I talking now?

This part of the discussion starts socially and finishes professionally. The better you know someone, the quicker alignment can happen. It can be as fast as 'Hi Sam, how are you?' If Sam looks grumpy and harassed, it may be worth seeing what is chewing him up: if it is a bad time to talk, let Sam sort his problems out and fix another time to meet.

At first meetings, alignment takes time and effort. They will be keen to know who you are and, bluntly, if it is worth talking to you. Making a formal pitch about your credentials may be necessary, but can backfire. They may be unimpressed, or they may dislike your boasting. Either way, it puts you in the position of a supplicant and them in the position of judge and jury: it is not a partnership discussion. The better way of doing this is to find some common background: places you have worked, people you both know, conferences attended. These professional links are a chance to show that you know what you are talking about. Do not get into a bragging contest about who has the best experience. Use the opportunity to flatter and soothe an executive ego: be suitably impressed by what they claim to have achieved and the challenges they have faced. Even areas of social overlap such as past times build some mutual respect.

Once the other side is comfortable that they are talking to the right person at the right time, you can move explicitly to the main subject of discussion.

When we got to the bank the meeting started with the formal exchange of *meishi* (business cards). We quickly found we had many areas of common background and experience: we had identified some areas from our research. They had identified some areas from our advance materials. It was a social chat which confirmed to them that we might know what we were talking about. Once they were relaxed we outlined how we wanted to run the meeting: we laid out an agenda and objective which demanded that they participate rather than we present. This was the expectation that we had set, and they were happy to humour us. We made no presentation at all.

Agree the problem/opportunity

If you can both agree on the problem or opportunity, the chances are that the solution will be relatively easy to find. In many cases, persuasive conversations go wrong because the two sides have different views about what the problem or opportunity is. Invest time to agree the problem explicitly. Even if you both agree the problem in broad outline, the chances are that you will have different perspectives on it. Explore these perspectives. You do not need to persuade at this moment: you need to listen.

If the conversation later on goes wrong, come back to this point: reaffirm what it is that you are trying to accomplish together. This step is the logical choke-point of the conversation. If in doubt, always come back to this point to clarify and confirm.

In the case of the Tokyo bank, this was the critical step. We had to reframe the problem for them. They had framed the problem as cutting costs. We knew this was unlikely: banking was growing, and firing people in Japan is as close as you can get to corporate suicide. So we got the bank to talk about their business. They proudly told us it was growing. We chatted about how one Western firm had reneged on some employment offers: they agreed that such employment practices would be a disaster for them. Slowly we let them discover that they did not want to cut costs: they wanted to keep costs steady while trading volumes rose. This is a radical reformulation of the problem leading to radically different solutions. As soon as we had made this breakthrough with them, we were winning. Simply by helping them reframe the problem, we had added huge amounts of credibility and value to them. And we had not shown them any paper or made any presentations: we had simply chatted. But it was very structured and purposeful chat.

Explore benefits and outcomes

Once you have agreed the problem or opportunity, a huge bear trap opens up. It is tempting to suggest the solution and discuss how it works. This may well lead to resistance. Humans are risk-averse. As you enthusiastically talk about what happens next, the other person will be imaging all the risks and hard work which your idea presents to them. Suddenly, you will find yourself on the defensive again, having to deal with all the demons which have been conjured up. The chances are that so many demons will emerge that the other person will mentally give up on your idea.

After you have agreed the nature of the problem or opportunity, show that it is worth fixing. Size the prize. If the prize is big enough, then it becomes worth taking on some risk and dealing with the demons. The bigger the prize, the more effort it is worth. So set expectations as high as you can at this stage: you can always backtrack from them later. It is much harder to raise expectations later. Anchor the discussion at the right level.

For the Tokyo bank this was a simple step. We had already reframed the problem: it was not about cutting absolute costs, but keeping costs stable during growth. All we had to do now was to size the prize: how much growth did they expect at zero cost increase over how long? We did not tell them: we let them discuss and agree this. Having framed the desired outcome, we got them to put a value on the outcome. When they estimated the annual benefits at over $8 million a year, they started to reframe their own expectations about the scale of the project. They did not need a little advice: they needed serious support to drive major profit improvement. They successfully sold themselves a larger engagement.

Outline the solution

With clear benefits agreed, it is finally possible to start discussing how to achieve them.

You will have a preferred solution: this is your desired outcome. But be flexible. Have a Plan A, B and C. You need to avoid a win/lose discussion where you press your case and the other party shows why it will not work. If you offer a choice you change the terms of debate: you are no longer saying 'my way or no way'. You set up a partnership discussion in which you are finding the best solution together. The simplest version of this is the three-choice trick:

- Choice A: very big and exciting, but you know is going to be too much and too risky
- Choice B: this is the choice you prefer
- Choice C: low-risk, low effort but really does not get anyone anywhere.

Let the other person tell you in no uncertain terms why A and C are useless choices. Let them confirm to themself their wisdom, business judgement and superiority. You can then profess your great thanks to them for guiding you to Choice B, which you wanted all along.

Instead of presenting our solution to the Tokyo bank, we let them discover it. By discovering the solution, the client owned it and believed it in a way that would never have happened if we had presented them with a pre-packaged solution. This was not a random conversation: it was structured and directed. We asked the client to complete a project logic with us in the meeting. The project logic had four elements, in order:

1. Desired outcomes (one or two key goals). In their case it was growth at no cost while maintaining or improving quality.
2. Key success factors: to achieve this outcome, what needs to be in place? (e.g. effective IT systems, clear processes, revamped skills, measures and rewards and more besides)
3. So where would we need to be in two months' time if we have made a good start? This is where they designed the project start with us.

4 What do we need to do now to set the project up for success? This was our guide to managing the decision-making process and politics.

By now the client had not only agreed to a project logic, but they had also emotionally committed to the project. It was their project, not just a consultant's project.

Pre-empt and resolve outstanding problems

This is the 'yes but....' part of the conversation. People start to say things like 'yes, but have you thought of.....' or 'I agree, but how about...'. Remember that everything before 'but' is baloney. They are raising their anxieties and concerns. There are many ways of dealing with these concerns. Probably the worst way is to argue your case: the smarter you are, the more you will drive the other person into a corner. Argument simply generates more argument.

> Argument simply generates more argument

Typically, objections come in three flavours:

- The constructive concern: This is where people identify a risk and try to solve it with you. Be open, be supportive, discuss options and find the resolution that works for both of you.

- The defensive objection: Where people raise concerns and do not engage in solutions, you have lost them. Do not fuel the argument by battling them into submission. Show that you have understood their concerns and you will take them on board. Reconfirm step 3: agree the problem and opportunity. And suggest another time when you can come back to work out a way of achieving a sensible solution. This gives them a victory and emotionally lets them believe you are on their side. When you next see them, you will have found out enough to know how to repackage and represent the same idea to them in a more palatable way and they will be more open to agreement: having won once they will have no need to keep on kicking you. If you cannot fix another meeting, still go back to step 3 and rebuild from there. Let them do the talking.

- The knee-jerk reaction: Sometimes people object because they feel they have to. If you take this objection too seriously you cause yourself problems. Let the objection go: offer a little sympathy, a joke or some distraction: do not engage in an argument. For instance, one store manager objected that an order for 20 cases of toothpaste was too much 'But', I said, 'there are only 12 tubes of toothpaste in each case, against 48 bars of soap in a case of soap.' It was utterly irrelevant detail, but the buyer felt he had been heard and had been given an excuse for saying 'yes', which he duly did.

The easiest way through this part of the conversation is to be open. Let them raise their concerns. Acknowledge them and then discuss them openly: let them find the solution. The biggest enemy here is the single-point solution. If there is only one possible solution, then you run the risk of a win–lose argument: you argue for the solution and they argue why it will not work. It is a destructive game to play. Open up different possibilities: then you have a partnership discussion in which you are working together to find the best (or least bad) solution.

For the Tokyo bank this was simple. Any objections they had were not to our project. They were simply raising concerns about achieving the goals they had set themselves. Every concern they raised became another concern for the project to resolve: they were creating an ever greater project for us.

Close and follow-up

Never assume that you have agreement. Most managers are not great at telepathy. They will not know exactly what you want.

Many people fall at this final hurdle. For instance, I was recently called in to see a government minister. I prepared thoroughly and it all went well. But I had been so focused on getting through the meeting that I had forgotten the most important thing of all: the close and the next steps. Government ministers have other things on their mind and do not have time to waste trying to work out what you are thinking or hoping for. You have to ask and be clear about what you want. Do not turn your golden opportunity into fool's gold.

> most managers are not great at telepathy

Confirm your agreement: what you think has happened may not be the same as what the other person thinks has happened. There are four main ways of closing the conversation. In the first three cases you get positive confirmation that you both understand what you have agreed:

- The direct close: 'So would you like to buy the car?' Very clear, but risky: you invite the answer 'no', in which case you get to start over again.

- The alternate close: 'Would you like to buy the silver car or blue car?' This is a sneaky close. You appear to be offering a choice, but you are not offering the choice of 'no'. Many people find it hard to resist this close.

- The action close: 'Here are the keys, I'll get the paperwork and as soon as you sign you can drive off.' This close has momentum built in which is hard to resist, and it is very clear.

- The assumed (confirmation) close: 'So we are all agreed that we will buy a fleet of pink-and-yellow-striped mini vans.' This is the sort of close used by chairmen at the end of meetings to summarise discussion. It takes a brave person to defy this close. But because it lacks positive confirmation from other people, there is a danger of this agreement unravelling later behind closed doors.

Once you have agreement, follow up. Fast. The longer you leave it, the more the agreement will go cold and second thoughts will start coming up. If possible, make the agreement public: once committed in public, people find it hard to backtrack. Send an email thanking them for their contribution and confirming the next steps: copy it to some relevant and interested parties. Ideally, give both parties a next step. You can show professionalism by following up. By asking for a next step from the other person you reinforce your mutual agreement and their commitment.

By the time we got to this stage, the Tokyo bank was ready to do the closing for us. One of the clients turned to us and asked: 'Have we just designed your project for you?'

'Yes,' I replied, 'do you like it?'

'Of course!' said the client. They had done the selling for us. They had designed the project, so they owned it and were committed to it. We then quickly agreed next steps for moving ahead. As soon as we got back to the office we did not celebrate. We debriefed, followed up on our commitments. And then we celebrated.

Summary

The invisible structure behind the persuasive conversation has seven simple steps:

1 Preparation

2 Alignment

3 Agree the problem or opportunity

4 Explore benefits and outcomes

5 Outline solutions

6 Pre-empt/resolve problems

7 Close.

Apply this structure consistently and contentious discussions become cooperative, negative outcomes become positive and passive agreements become active support.

The persuasive conversation, like most influencing skills, is most effective when it is invisible. People should not feel that they are being persuaded or influenced. Gently guide them in the right direction. Let them discover the right answer. Done well, they will think it is their own idea. They will commit willingly to the idea, whereas active persuading often leads to no more than passive and grudging agreement. Influencers go beyond that to build active and lasting support.

Chapter 13

Conclusions: the mindset and myths of influence

nfluence is like air: it is both invisible and essential. As the world shifts from traditional command-and-control hierarchies to networks which depend on each other, so influence becomes ever more important. Because it is invisible, it is both ignored and misunderstood. This represents a wonderful opportunity for the few people who both understand influence and acquire it. They are competing against non-existent competition. And where there is competition, influencers learn to convert opposition into support.

> Influence is like air: it is both invisible and essential

It is too simplistic to reduce influence to three handy tips, or a one-minute magic formula for success. Learning influence, like learning a sport or a musical instrument, takes time and effort. But to start the journey to influence, it helps to have some guiding principles. The high-level map for the journey to influence has three parts:

- The mindset of influence: how influencers think and operate
- Learning the art of influence
- The myths of influence: the traps to avoid on the journey.

The mindset of influence

Influence is invisible because it is about how people think. We cannot see people's thoughts. Thoughts drive behaviour, which drives actions and results. We can look at the results that influential people achieve but still have no idea about what makes them influential. Just as we cannot understand a person by looking at their shadow, we cannot understand influence by looking at its effect. We have to look for the causes of influence, not at its symptoms.

Over 60 skills and principles of influence are outlined in this book. Behind those skills lie four ways of thinking which separate effective influencers from the rest of us. Thinking like an influencer is the first and most important step to becoming an influencer. We can use and adapt these four principles to suit our own style. We do not need to sell our soul or clone our brain to become influential. We do not need to become someone else. We simply need to build on the best of who we already are.

The four ways of influential thinking are:

1 Be ambitious
2 Walk in other people's shoes
3 Build commitment
4 Start at the end.

Be ambitious

Lack of ambition is a recipe for a quiet life in the backwaters of underachievement. For many people, the greatest barrier to success is in their heads. They accept low expectations for themselves. Low expectations are always self-fulfilling. Ambitious people have high expectations of themselves and others. They reach for the stars. Even if they fail and only reach the moon, they will be far ahead of others whose expectations reach no further than next year's beach vacation. The world has never been changed by unambitious people.

> The world has never been changed by unambitious people

Ambitious people are not satisfied with the status quo. They want to change things and make things happen.

Ambition which is all 'me ... me... me' is not influential. It leads to conflict and fails to build networks of trust and support. Ambition which is 'we ... we ... we' is influential. It stretches people and teams, and builds commitment and camaraderie. The mindset of ambition is both positive and opportunity-focused.

Ambition can make influential people uncomfortable to work with. They can be driven, focused and intense in a way that less influential people find intimidating. They often appear to be unreasonable: they will stretch people and ask them to do more than they thought possible. Stretching people can build, not wreck, relationships. When people are stretched, they grow and develop and are proud of what they have achieved. That builds loyalty to the person that led them to exceed their own expectations. Stretch is ineffective when it leads to stress, not pressure. The great dividing line between stress and pressure is control: people under pressure who still have control over their fate can perform exceptionally well. People under pressure who have no control over events quickly discover stress and burnout.

Walk in other people's shoes

We all like to think we are the centre of the universe. Influencers may also think that they are the centre of the universe, but they do not always show it. They work hard to see the world through the eyes of each person they want to influence. They are always asking themselves difficult questions:

- Why should this person want to talk to me?
- Why should they want to follow or support me?
- What do they want, what do they not want – how can I use that to my advantage?
- How can I find out more about this person?

● What other choices do they have, why should they prefer my way?

Walking in other people's shoes is not about being nice to other people, or even agreeing with them. It is about understanding them. Once we understand someone we can start to play their tune.

The core skill for walking in other people's shoes is very simple: listen actively. Good influencers have two ears and one mouth, and use them in that proportion. We can only understand other people if we listen to them. Given that most people enjoy talking about their favourite subject, themselves, the simple act of listening builds rapport at the same time as building our knowledge of the people we want to influence.

Listening helps separate influence from persuasion. Persuaders will often be skilled at talking and can persuade someone to buy something or do something once. **Influencers play for far higher stakes than persuaders.** Influencers play for far higher stakes than persuaders. Where persuaders gain a one-off commitment, influencers build lasting commitment. Influence is an expensive commitment of time and effort, which pays very good dividends for a very long time.

Build commitment

The commitment mindset is central to the world of influence, not control. The control mindset likes hierarchy: power comes from position. This makes it very limiting: the control mindset does not reach beyond the barriers of the hierarchy to make things happen outside a limited range of control. The controlling mindset is enabled by the organisation, but also limited by it. The controlling mindset thinks that commitment is a one-way street: anyone lower in the organisation must show commitment to people higher in the organisation. Teamwork for a controlling manager means 'My way or no way': if you do not obey than you are not a good team player.

The commitment mindset is not constrained by hierarchy or by the formal limitations of power. The commitment mindset builds a network of informal alliances which enables the influencer to achieve things far beyond the dreams of the controlling mindset. Commitment is a two-way street based on mutual obligations. Building commitment takes time and skill. These skills form the heart of influence, outlined in this book. Underlying the whole commitment process is trust: influencers have to be trusted if they are to succeed. The trust equation is a simple shorthand for working out how strong each relationship is, and what needs to be done to strengthen it. For the record, the trust equation is:

$$T = (VxC)/(RxD)$$

In plain English: trust is built by sharing similar values (V) and building credibility (C), which comes from delivering on promises. Risk is destroyed by distance (D): the greater the distance between what I say and do, between my values and yours, the less the trust. It is also limited by risk (R): the greater the risk, the more trust is required. However, risk is relative: show that your risky idea is less risky than doing nothing, then suddenly your idea starts to look more attractive.

There is a hard edge to the commitment mindset. The influencer may be generous, reliable, committed and adaptable in the quest to build trusted partnerships. But the influencer always expects something in return, and sets that expectation from the start of the relationship. Partnership means give and take. Bowing to the wishes of other people is

trust and respect are more valuable currencies than popularity

the road to popularity and to weakness. Influencers learn that trust and respect are more valuable currencies than popularity.

Start at the end

There is an old tale of a traveller who is lost in Ireland. He asks a local for directions to Dublin and is told: 'If I was going to Dublin … I wouldn't start from here.' We are where we are and we have to make the most of it. But from this truism comes another which grannies and gurus trot out at regular intervals: 'first things first'. This is a catastrophic piece of advice. It implies that we start with what we have and proceed from there.

Instead of starting with what we have, influential people start at the end. They work out the desired goal and then work back from there. They map the journey from the destination back to today. If we start from where we are, we may decide that our goal (Dublin or any other goal) is not achievable. If we start at the end, the only question we should ask is 'how do we get there?' not 'can we get there?'

Starting at the end is a mindset which consistently drives different and more effective behaviour. It is focused on the future not the past, on action not analysis and on outcomes not on process. The mindset shows itself in the questions asked in common day-to-day situations:

- *Crises*: 'how do we move forward?' not 'what went wrong and who can I blame?'
- *Conflicts*: 'what are we arguing about and is it worth it?' not 'how do I win?'
- *Meetings*: 'what will we achieve in this meeting?' not 'what is the formal agenda?'
- *Project planning*: 'what is our goal?' not 'what is the process and where is the risk log?'
- *Presentations*: 'what is my key message and for who?' not 'can we prepare another 50 PowerPoint slides, just in case we get a question?'

Starting at the end requires firmness about the goals but flexibility about the means. This flexibility makes it much easier to adapt to other people and to build commitment. People who are stuck in the control way of thinking lack such flexibility: they hope that strict compliance with a process will yield the right outcome. They use the same map, whatever their journey may be. However hard they run, they never make progress: they simply cover the same course faster. Starting at the end ensures the influencer chooses a worthwhile destination. They may not always travel the fastest, but at least they make progress.

Learning the art of influence

Everyone acquires skills and habits which help them make things happen and be productive. Think about how you have acquired the skills and habits that shape how you work. I have asked this of thousands of executives and I give them a choice of six ways of learning: pick the two most productive sources of learning that have helped shape how you operate:

- Books
- Courses
- Bosses
- Peers
- Role models
- Experience.

Typically, no one chooses books or courses, which could be awkward for someone who writes books and offers courses. But that is reality. We learn mainly from personal experience and the experience of those around us. At an emotional level it is more credible than any theory in a book. Rationally, it is more relevant to our immediate environment. But if that is how we learn, then our learning is a random walk. We bump into good experiences and role models, we learn good lessons. We bump into poor experiences and role models and we learn lessons which send us into a swamp of bad practice.

It is not possible to start any book on page one and become the perfect leader, footballer or influencer by the time we finish the last page. That is not the purpose of this book. The purpose of this book is to take some of the randomness out of the random walk of experience. By offering structure and a new perspective a book can accelerate our learning from experience and guide us away from negative lessons to more positive lessons.

By learning from experience we can build our own style and our own way of being influential. Influence is not a recipe which bakes everyone into the same sort of cake. It does not try to change you into someone else. It simply offers you the chance to make the most of who you already are.

No one can hope to learn all 60 skills and principles at once. Focus on one or two skills to start with. Practise and experiment with them. Build them into your personal repertoire of skills, and then move on to the next skills. Starting with active listening is simple, discreet and effective. But choose what works for you.

This book gives you a framework for understanding and acquiring influence. Used well, a framework is like scaffolding: it helps you build your talent the way you want it to grow. Used poorly, a framework is like a prison from which there is no escape. The difference is in how you choose to interpret the book. If you use the book as a mandatory formula to be followed, the frameworks become a prison. Use the book as a guide to principles which you adapt for your needs, and the frameworks become scaffolding to help you build. The scaffolding versus prisons choice is the same one that all books and courses offer.

Influence: the one sin and four myths

The subjects of influence and power are shrouded in mystery and much misunderstood. Although they are essential skills to making things happen in organisations, they are often seen as slightly grubby topics. Managers are comfortable learning about things like accounting and marketing. But learning about influence and power sounds devious, divisive and self-interested. This is unfortunate, because influence and power are central to making organisations work.

One cardinal sin

The bedrock of influence is trust. Most leaders forgive most sins. They know that mistakes happen and disasters occur. They can forgive bad jokes, bad dress and occasionally bad judgement. The one thing most bosses find unforgivable is breach of trust. Once a boss no longer trusts a team member, it is game over. It may take weeks or months, but eventually the boss and team member will part ways. Equally, few team members want to work with a boss they do not trust, even if they like the boss personally. Peers have a choice about who they collaborate with: trust plays a central part in that choice.

Without trust it becomes very hard to build alliances, commitment and support across the firm. There is much more to being an effective influencer than trust, but lack of trust is a killer. Breaking trust is not just a matter of undermining a colleague or a boss. It also includes bad-mouthing people behind their backs; breaking perceived promises and commitments; not being honest or misleading people; failing to support an ally or a boss at a critical moment. All of these are betrayals: even if what you did was technically correct, the sense of betrayal will remain. Shattered trust is like shattered glass: it is very hard to rebuild.

The Machiavelli myth

The art of influence and power is not about Machiavellian politics. Plotting against colleagues, stabbing people in the back and being devious is not the way to gain power and influence. Effective influence is based on trust.

There is a calculating element to influence: you have to know where and when to invest precious time and effort in building your alliances. There is also a ruthless element to influence: knowing when to seize the moment and take control of an agenda. This kind of calculation and ruthlessness is a benign force for the individual and the firm. Everyone benefits when you make the right investments and manage the right agenda. Influence is not, however, about being nice, as we will see in the friendship myth below.

The friendship myth

Influence is not about being liked and making friends. Influence is based on alliances of common interests and trust. Eventually, a professional alliance may become a personal friendship. The goal is to create a productive alliance, not to make a personal friend-

> Influence is not about being liked

ship. The friendship myth is important because it is natural for people to seek popularity. This simply leads to weakness: pandering to other people's demands and dancing to whatever the mood music of the day might be. Influential relationships are based on partnerships, not friendships. Partners act as equals: they work towards common goals and hopefully share a common understanding of how things should work.

The morality myth

Some people see influence as evil and manipulative: they want influence to have morals and to be a force for good. Influence does not have morals. It is neither moral nor immoral: it is amoral. It is a

> Influence does not have morals

force for good or a force for evil, depending on who uses it and for what purposes. In other words, influence is as moral as the influencer who uses the skills of influence. Hopefully you will use influence as a force for good: knowing how influence works, you will better resist influence when it is in the wrong hands. That is your choice.

The magic myth

Successful influencers seem to have an aura of magic about them. Everyone wants to get a bit of their magic pixie dust. Like charisma, influence is treated as something you either have or do not have. Because effective influencing is invisible to third parties, it appears to be even more magical and mysterious. The simple message of *How to Influence* is that there is no magic to influence: or if there is, this book has decoded the spell. In place of magic there are a series of skills, behaviours and mindsets that all managers can acquire to become influential. As you build these skills you will slowly master the invisible art of influence. Colleagues will start to wonder how you make things happen so easily, how you seem to find the right opportunities, how you turn crises into opportunities and why so many people help you. Whether you choose to share the secret of your magic will be for you to decide.

Acknowledgements

One of the main messages of *How to Influence* is that we can only succeed with and through other people. We all need a web of influence and support to make anything happen, including writing a book. This book is the product of a huge range of influences and influencers to whom I am hugely grateful.

This book is based heavily on experience of working across Asia, Europe and North America in most industries. So my first debt is to all those organisations which have tolerated my presence for anything from years to days. They include:

Accenture, AIG, AGM, Airbus, American Express, Apple Computers, Armstrong Industries, Aviva, BAT, Barclays Bank, Cap Gemini, Chase Group, CISCO, Citibank, Cognitas, Diatech, *First* magazine, Future Leaders, Hallmark Cards, HBOS, HCA, HMRC (Inland Revenue), ICI, Lloyds Bank, LLUK, Merita Nordbanken, Merrill Lynch, MetLife, Mitsubishi Chemicals, Monsanto, National Commercial Bank, National Air Traffic Service, Natwest, Netfoods, Norwegian Dairy Association, People's Choice, Philip Reynolds, Philips, Procter & Gamble, RHM, Royal Sun Alliance, SABIC, San Miguel, SDP, Skype, Start Up, SWIFT, Symantec, Teach First, Teaching Leaders, Thorn Rental, UBS, Union Carbide, Zurich Financial Services.

Influence is, above all, about individuals, not institutions. I have been influenced by a huge array of people who have been generous with the most valuable resource of all: time.

Philip Kotler of Kellogg business school has both given support and made critical interventions for me at key stages which have made a huge difference, as has James Kelly over a period of decades. Jon Huggett not only volunteered to do some implausible book research for me, but has been a steady intellectual check and balance for me. Shani Ospina and Laura Watkins at Cognitas are role models for the power of mindsets; Stephen Manbridge at AGM is a role model for the three E's of energy, enthusiasm and excitement from which all managers can learn.

The book itself would not have come about without a veritable army of support and influence. Back in the mists of time Tony Johnson provoked me into writing books: so it is all your fault, Tony. At Pearson I have been fortunate to have the support of an outstanding team. Richard Stagg fatally encouraged me to write the book; Samantha Jackson epitomised patience and professionalism in editing this book. Caroline Jackson, Laura Blake, Daniel Culver and Lucy Blackmore brought the book to market.

Finally, my thanks to my whole family who have endured obsessive mutterings and rantings as I wrote the book: Gaie, Toby, Jane and Hiromi have been a constant source of comfort, support and influence.

If, despite this cornucopia of support, there are still faults with this book then they can only be mine.

Index

A

acting the part
  ambition 90–92
  behaviour, influential 85–90
  looking the part 92–95
  perception management 83–84
  success, rules of 84–85
active listening
  common mistakes 111
  contradiction principle 103,
    108–9
  disclosure 103, 109–11
  EAR response (Empathise,
    Agree, Resolve) 197
  effective 102–3
  farming *versus* hunting mindset
    102
  other people's shoes, walking in
    246
  paraphrasing 103, 106–8
  questions, purposeful 103–5,
    110
  reinforcement 103, 105–6, 110
  as sales technique 101–2
advice, asking for 55–56
agenda control 16–17, 29
  administrative chores 29–30
  control, taking 29–30
  stress, using 29
  void, filling 31
ambition
  control 92
  influential thinking 244–45
  as strategy 91–92

unreasonable management, art
    of 92
archetypes 166–69
assignments
  alternative, considering 187,
    201–2
  enjoyment, and success
    199–200
  skills, building 201–2
authority
  dress codes 93–94
  versus influence 5–6

B

battles, picking
  assignments 187, 199–202
  budget negotiations 187,
    188–90
  common sense 207
  conflict management 187,
    193–96, 196–99
  crises, as opportunities 187,
    190–92
  dos and don'ts checklist 207
  new role, moving into 203–6
behaviour, influential
  energy, sustaining 88–89, 96
  engagement, with eyes and voice
    85–88, 96
  enthusiasm, and visualising
    success 89–90, 96
belonging
  esprit de corps, creating 62–64
  as essential 71–72

belonging *continued*
loyalty, sustaining 61–62
and meaning 62–67, 64
peer group *versus* boss pressure
64
recognition 64–67
and tribal instinct 62
Blair, Tony 131
blaming 190–91
blinding flash of the obvious
(BFO) 32, 205
bragging 134–35
budget negotiations
budget targets 187, 188
credibility, building 189–90
playing hardball 189–90
playing smartball 190
repetition, and building
consensus 189
strike early 188–89
business plans 17–18
business relationships
boss to team member 129
colleague to colleague 129
team member to boss 129
team work, effective 130

C
calculation 251–52
CEOs (Chief Executive Officers)
home country bias 23–24,
146–47
key influencing techniques
15–16
as kings of corporate world
18–19
claims to fame 16
complex firms 26
promotions 26–27
sponsorship 27
voluntary exile, consequences of
27–29
Clinton, Bill 155
colleagues, understanding
personality tests 174–76
perspective, changing 182

psychotherapy 163
style compass 43, 176–81
see also scripts
command and control, break
down of 4–5
commitment, building
agreements, publicising 74–76
control, giving 68–71, 246–47
generosity 117, 124
the hook 50–58
initiation rites, brutal public
71–72
mutual commitment 58–60
partnership 247
persuasion *versus* influence 49,
181–82
private disagreements 73–74
public commitments 72–73
respect 247
'right choreography' 75–76
time and effort 77
tribe, building 61–67, 71–72
trust equation 247
common sense 207
compliance culture 69
conflict management 187
alliance, turning hostility into
138
calming down 197–98
cold wars 193
detachment, techniques for
198–99
EAR response (Empathise,
Agree, Resolve) (listening)
196
FEAR response (Fight, Engage,
Argue, Retaliate) 196
Nelson doctrine 195–96
organisations, and conflict 193
private disagreements 73–74
war, conditions of 193–95
way forward, agreeing 198
conformity
dress codes 94, 98
partnership principle 131–32
values alignment 146–47,
158–59

contradiction principle
  active listening 103, 108–9
  commitment 56–57
control, giving
  commitment culture, moving to
    68–70, 246–47
  delegation 70–71
  self-control 68–70
  worker decisions 70
creativity 220–21
credibility
  bragging 134–35
  competitiveness 134
  credentials, laying out 134
  expertise, sharing 135
  follow-up 135
  insight, showing 135
  listening 135
  resumes 134
  smart questions 135
  and trust 133–34
crises
  denial and blaming 190–91
  leading 190
  as opportunities 187, 244
  partnership principle 137–38
  successful responses 191–92
cynicism 89

D
delegation 70–71
denial 190–91
diversity
  versus conformity 146–47,
    158–59
  versus intimacy 131
dress codes
  aspiration 95
  authority 93–94
  conformity 94, 98
  conservatism 94–95

E
employer, choice of
  global firms 22–24
  influence 22

networks 41–42
  status 21–22
endorsements, power of 16, 17–18
energy, sustaining 88–89, 96
enthusiasm, and success 89–90,
    96
expectations, managing 151, 233
experience, learning from 249–50
eyes
  eye contact, power of 85–87,
    106
  watching people 85–86

F
fame *see* claims to fame
first impressions
  first meetings 95–96
  presentations, making 96–98
  selfless, being 136

G
generosity
  commitment, building 117, 124
  customised, not generic 116,
    117–20
  earned, not unearned 116,
    120–21
  measured, not unlimited 116,
    121–22
  popularity 115–16
  principles of 116
  requested, not unrequested
    116, 122–24
  self-interest 115, 124
  thanks 136–37, 156
global teams, and contradiction
    principle 57
Gono, Gideon 164
gossip 182
Graham, Billy 86

H
HBOS 191
hierarchy 3–4, 6, 131, 246–47
hook, and commitment
  advice, asking for 55–56

hook, and commitment *continued*
  contradiction principle 56–57
  personal introductions 50,
      51–52, 53
  problem solution offers 50,
      52–54
  targeted networking 51–52
  teasers 50, 54, 55

I
induction process 71
initiation rites 71–72
introductions, personal 50, 51–52,
    53
invisibility, of influence 6, 159,
    239, 244

J
John Timpson 67

K
Kevin Bacon game 51
Kissinger, Henry 195–96

L
learning, sources of 249–50
listening *see* active listening
looking the part
  appearances, judging by 92–95
  dress codes 93–95, 98
loyalty 61–64
Luther King, Martin 87–88

M
MB/TI (Myers-Briggs Type
      Indicators) 175–76
meetings 244
  agreements, publicising 74–76
  new ideas, killing 73–74
  paraphrasing 107–8
  relaxing 89
meishi (business cards) 21, 231
mentoring relationships 20,
    119–20
Microsoft 25

mirroring
  body movements 86–87
  conformity 94, 98
Moore, Paul 191
myths, of influence
  friendship myth 252
  Machiavelli myth 251–52
  magic myth 252
  morality myth 252

N
negotiation
  interests, not positions 212,
      213, 214–15
  options, offering 212, 214,
      216–17
  public private partnerships 212,
      219–20
  soup story illustration 212–13
  story, crafting 212, 214, 218–19
  symbolic concessions 212,
      217–18, 221
Nelson, Admiral 195–96
'nemawashi' 75–76
networks
  absence of, in new role 35–36
  employer, switching 41–42
  headhunters 36
  influence checklist 43–46
network effect 36
  power, locus of 37, 38
  power web, mapping 39–41, 43
  resources 37
  technocrats 37
  trading partners 38
new role, moving into
  networks, absence of 35–36
  script, writing own 203
  team, picking right 205–6
  vision, as story 204–5

O
objections, dealing with 235–36
organisations
  and conflict 193

flat 5
as source of power 21
Orwell, George 155

P
partnership principle
    alliance, turning hostility into
        138
    business relationships 129–30
    conflict 138
    credibility 133–36
    crises 137–38
    humans, not roles 130–31
    partner, acting like 131–33
    patronage, power of 20
    selfless, being 136–37
perceptions
    management of 83–84
    versus reality 218–19
    and trust 144–45
Perrier 191
personality tests 174–76
persuasion, *versus* influence 7–8
persuasive conversations
    alignment 226, 230–31
    benefits and outcomes,
        exploring 226, 233
    closing 236–38
    emotional engagement principle
        227
    follow-up 238
    invisibility of 239
    logic principle 228
    noddy principle 227
    objections, dealing with 235–36
    options principle 228
    other people's shoes principle
        228, 230
    partnership principle 228
    preparation 226, 229–30
    problems, pre-empting/resolving
        226, 235–36
    questions, open *versus* closed
        104–5

as sales pitch 225
solutions, outlining 226,
    233–35
telepathy, managers not great at
    236–37
win-win principle 227
Peters, Tom 25
platform, building
    agenda control 16, 29–31
    claims to fame 16, 25–28
    employer, choice of 21–24, 22
    endorsements, power of 16,
        17–18
    function, choice of 21–24
    organisation, as source of power
        21
    patronage, power of 18–20
power web, mapping 39–41, 43
PowerPoint *see* presentations
praise, giving 60, 66–67
presentations 244
    first meetings 95–98
    partnership principle 132–33
pressure *versus* stress 92
Proctor & Gamble 3, 24
project logic 234–35
project planning 244
psychotherapy 163
public private partnerships 212,
    219–20

Q
questions, open *versus* closed
    104–5, 110

R
rapport 106
recognition, giving 117–20, 124
reinforcement
    active listening 103, 105–6, 110
    value alignment 106, 147–49
relationships
    business 129–30
    divisive 40–41

relaxation 88–89
reputation 207
risk
    raising 151–53
    reducing 153–54
ruthlessness 251–52

S
scripts
    archetypes 166–69
    changing 173–74
    influence, as amoral 173
    luck, making own 174
    personal, understanding
        165–66, 170
    positive stories, constructing
        163–64
    self-reinforcing 173
    using to influence 170–72
self-control 68–70
self-interest 158
Semler, Richard 70
Skype 3
speeches 87–88
sponsorship 27
stories
    in negotiation 212, 214, 218–19
    and scripts 163–64
    and vision 204–5
stress
    versus pressure 92
    using 29
style compass 43
    actions 180–81
    behaviours, identifying 176–78
success
    and enjoyment 199–200
    rules of 84–85
    visualising 89–90
Sun Tsu doctrine 193–95

T
Teach First 63, 174
teams, effective 130, 205–6

thanks, giving 136–37, 156
time, giving 119–20, 124
TQM (total quality management)
        68–69
trust
    breaking 143, 251
    credibility 133–34, 149–51
    distance 154–59
    earning 145–46
    invisibility of 159
    misleading words, in business
        155–57
    overcommunication 157
    perceptions 144–45
    politicians 154–55
    risk 151–54
    taking for granted 143–44
    trust equation 146, 159, 247
    values alignment 146–49,
        158–59
    see also partnership principle
Tylenol 191

V
values alignment
    conformity *versus* diversity
        146–47, 158–59
    listening 148
    persuasive conversations 226,
        230–31
    respect 148–49
    worldviews, reinforcement of
        147–49
vision, as story 204–5
visualisation, and success 89–90
voice, using 87–88
voluntary exile, consequences of
        27–29

W
win-win approach
    creativity 220–21
    mind-set 220–21
    negotiation 212– 221
Wiseman, Richard 174